Word
Made Easy

A beginner's guide including how-to skills and projects

Ewan Arthur

ARCTURUS

Contents

How to use this book

This book will help you learn how to use Microsoft **Word**, probably the most popular word processor in the world.

- It is written for beginners and covers only what you really need.

- There's no jargon, just simple instructions and lots of pictures. You'll start with the basics and will soon be able to write letters, design posters and add pictures.

Step-by-step skills pages

These pages explain each skill and the steps needed to use the skill.

Pictures show you what's on your computer screen.

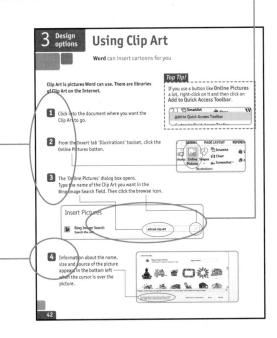

Project pages

These pages get you to practice the skills in a series of fun projects.

The projects are explained with step-by-step instructions and pictures.

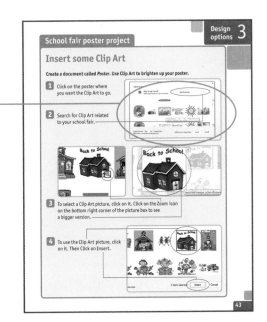

The Microsoft Office Word window

What you will see when you open a **Word** document:

The **Quick Access Toolbar** – does most of the very common tasks such as 'Open' and' Save', but without any options.

The **Ribbon** – where most of the options that you will learn about are found.

The **Close** button. Click to exit **Word**.

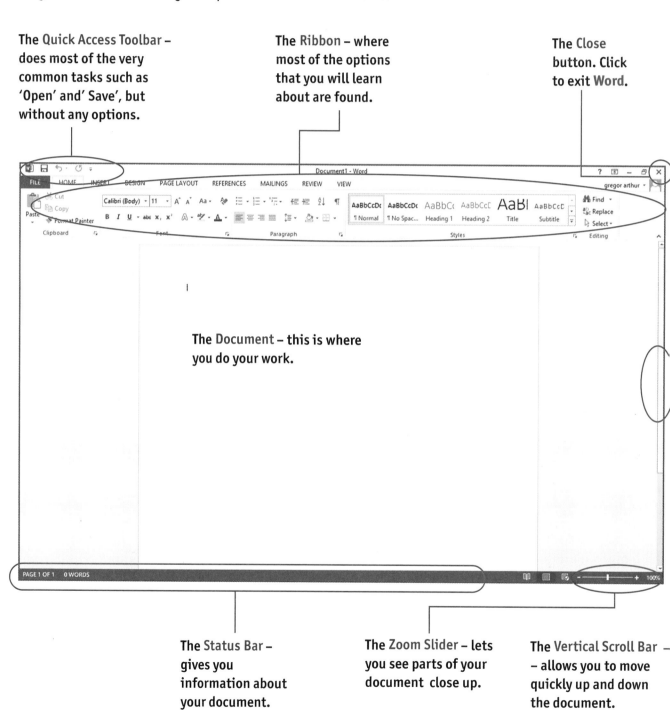

The **Document** – this is where you do your work.

The **Status Bar** – gives you information about your document.

The **Zoom Slider** – lets you see parts of your document close up.

The **Vertical Scroll Bar** – allows you to move quickly up and down the document.

The ribbon

The **ribbon** is where to find most of the tools you use. The ribbon is divided into **tabs**. Each tab is split up into sets of tools. **Word** is clever and depending on what you are doing, puts useful tabs in the ribbon.

The **File** tab – opens the backstage area, where you create and save your documents.

A **Button**.

A **Button Drop-down Menu** – shows options related to a button.

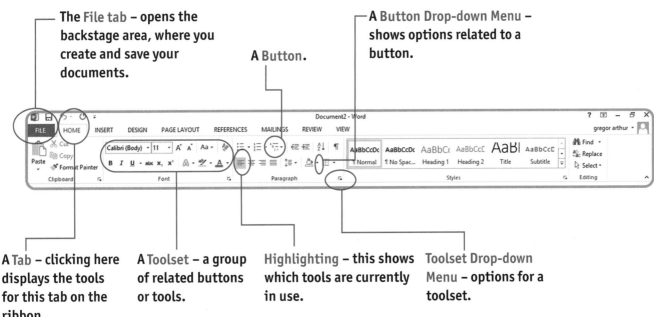

A **Tab** – clicking here displays the tools for this tab on the ribbon.

A **Toolset** – a group of related buttons or tools.

Highlighting – this shows which tools are currently in use.

Toolset Drop-down Menu – options for a toolset.

Starting Word

What to do to get **Word** running on your computer.

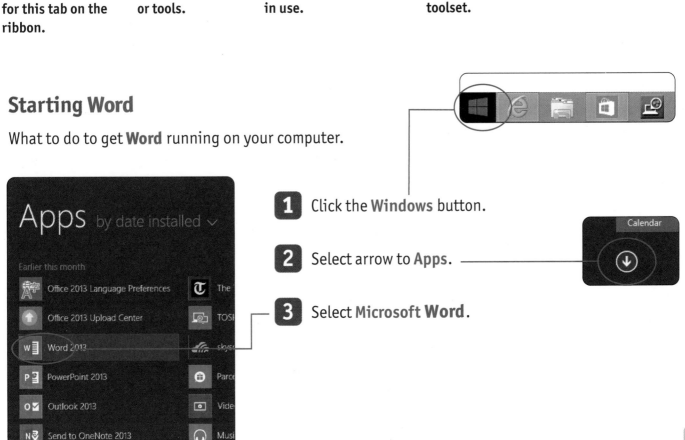

1 Click the **Windows** button.

2 Select arrow to **Apps**.

3 Select Microsoft **Word**.

Using the mouse

You will use a mouse and keyboard with **Word**. You can often use either to do the same thing. For example, get help by pressing the **F1** function key or clicking on the **?** icon.

Common terms and techniques

Right-click – press and release the <u>right</u>-hand button.

Click – press and release the <u>left</u>-hand button. Two quick clicks is a **Double-click**.

Click-and-drag – press the left mouse button, move (or drag) the cursor, then release it. This either highlights everything covered or moves whatever was selected by the first click.

Mouse pointer – moving the mouse moves the mouse pointer around the screen. It changes depending on what is going on.

Cursor – The flashing line (cursor) shows where type will appear when entered.

Hover-over – keep the mouse pointer over a button for a few seconds. This will often produce a pop-up message.

Using the keyboard

Common terms and techniques

Esc – closes any pop-up windows you don't want anymore.

Caps Lock – when pressed, everything is typed in capital letters.

Function Keys – can be used as shortcuts for tools and options. The **F7** key starts the spelling checker.

Backspace – deletes text to the <u>left</u> of the cursor.

Delete – deletes text to the <u>right</u> of the cursor.

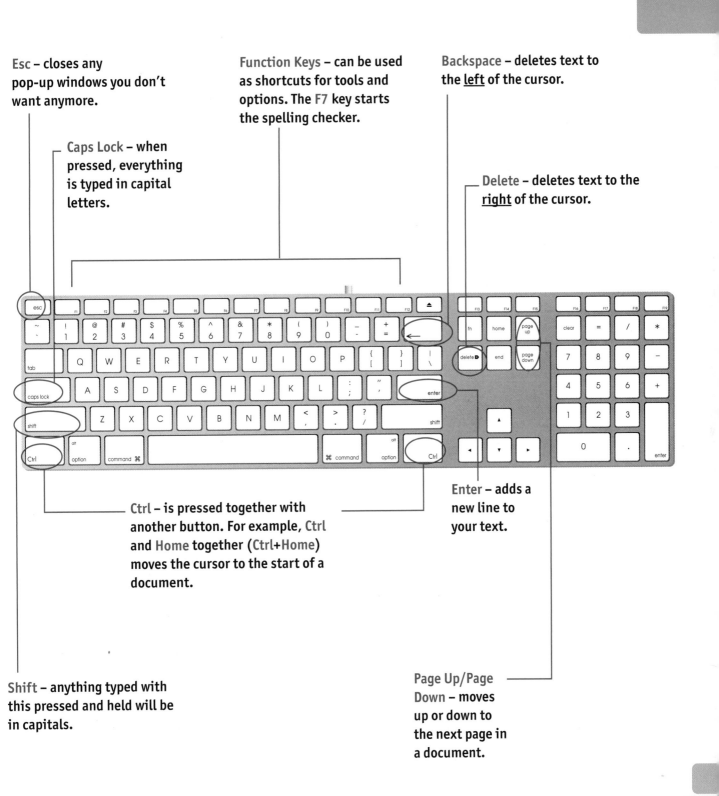

Ctrl – is pressed together with another button. For example, **Ctrl** and **Home** together (**Ctrl+Home**) moves the cursor to the start of a document.

Enter – adds a new line to your text.

Shift – anything typed with this pressed and held will be in capitals.

Page Up/Page Down – moves up or down to the next page in a document.

Word on touch screens

Word can work on a touch screen as well as a PC computer. You can change between **Mouse Mode** and **Touch Mode**. This will help make it easier to use touch-screen commands.

1 Click the **drop-down arrow** on the Quick Access toolbar.

2 Select **Touch/Mouse Mode** from the drop-down menu.

3 Select **Touch** from the drop-down menu.

4 The Ribbon switches to **Touch Mode**, and you will see more space around the buttons.

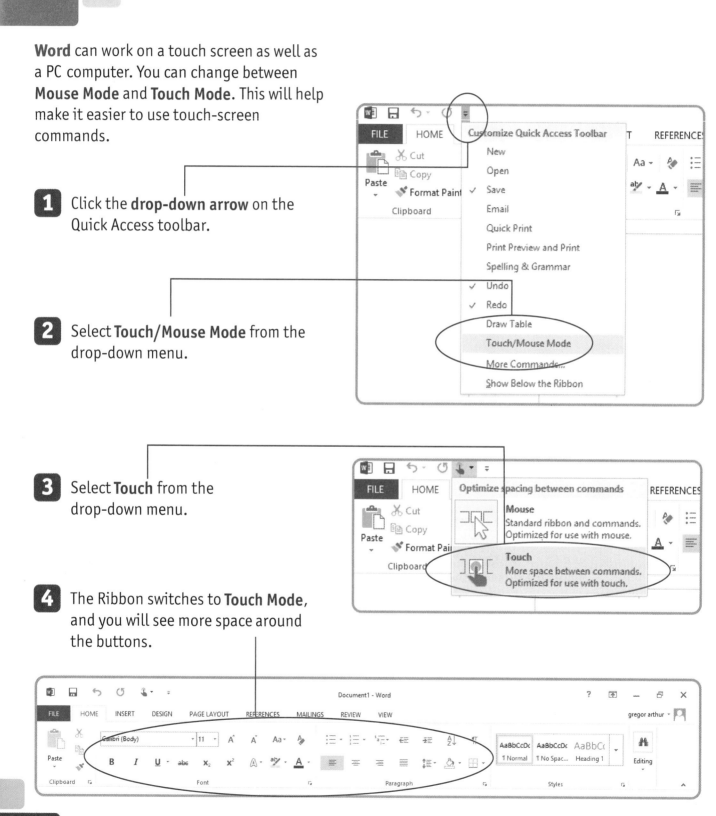

Common terms and techniques

There are different versions of **Word** for tablets. Here are three ways of interacting with a touch-screen device with your fingers.

Tapping

One tap on an item opens or activates it the same way a mouse click does.

Stretching

Touching the screen with two fingers and stretching them apart will zoom in, making things bigger.

Highlighting

Press to select a word and then slide to select more. You can copy words this way to paste somewhere else.

Launching Word

Creating and Saving documents

Start a new document and save it so you can use it again.

1 Launch **Word** and on the start screen click on **Blank document.**

2 A new document opens. Select the **File** tab.

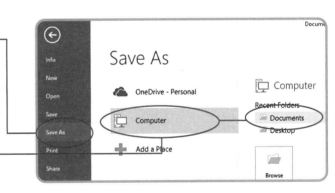

3 The backstage area opens. Click on **Save As** in the list. The 'Save As' window appears. Click on **Computer** and then **Documents.**

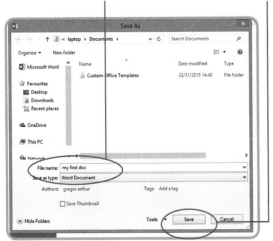

4 The 'Save As' dialog box opens. Type *my first doc* in the 'File name' field. Then click **Save.**

Top Tip!

This can be done from the 'Quick Access' Toolbar. Click the **New** and **Save** buttons.

Using folders

Open your documents and make a place to Save them

When you create a lot of documents it's good to organize them and keep copies as back-up.

1 Open **Word** again. Your new document is listed under 'Recent'. Click on it.

2 If the document is not in the 'Recent' list, click on **Open Other Documents**.

3 The 'Open' dialog box pops up, allowing you to find your file on your computer.

4 You can save it with a new name and/or save it in another folder. Folders allow you to organize your files. Use the **New Folder** button in the 'Save As' dialog box to create new folders.

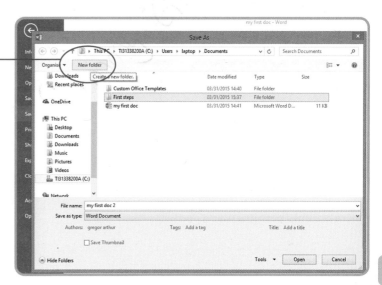

Getting about

Using the mouse and the keyboard

You can add, change or delete any part of your document by using the mouse or the keyboard.

Remember!

The flashing cursor is where your typing appears.

This is where the cursor is |but it should be flashing

1 To add text to a different part of the document, move the mouse pointer and click, or use the **Arrow** keys.

This is where the mouse pointer is when it is over the ⌶ text area

2 If you can't see the part where you want to type, click-and-drag the 'Scroll Bar' or use the **Page Up** and **Page Down** keys.

3 Use the **Backspace** key to delete text to the left of the cursor, or the **Delete** key to delete text to the right.

This is a block of text that has been selected by using click-and-drag

4 To delete a lot of text, click-and-drag the mouse pointer across the text, then press the **Delete** key.

Top Tip!

Ctrl + Home moves the cursor to the top of the document, and **Ctrl + End** to the end. **Ctrl + A** selects everything.

First steps project

Create and alter your document

Save a back-up of your document in a folder where you will find it easily.

1 Open your *my first doc* document, either from the 'Recent' list or the 'Open' dialog box.

> This is my first word document.

2 Type the words on to the page as shown.

3 Click on the 'File' tab and then **Close**.

4 Open your *my first doc* document again, then change the text as shown.

> I am writing a story.

5 Click on the **New Folder** button. A new folder appears in the dialog box and you can type in the name *My first story*, then press **Open**.

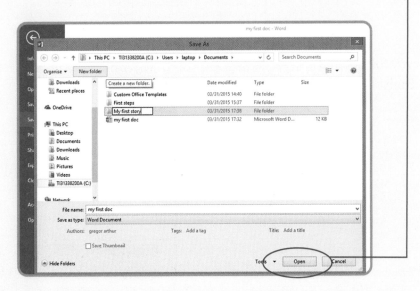

How you view your doc

You can move around, **Zoom** in, or change how many pages you see

The default zoom is 100% – **Word** is showing you what your document would look like if printed. But you might want it closer for more detail or further away to get the big picture.

1 Click the **View** tab.

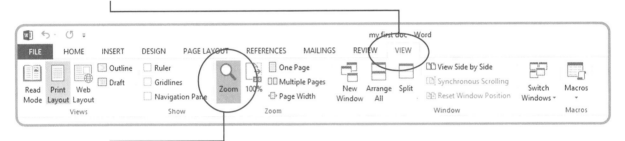

2 Click the **Zoom** button. The 'Zoom' dialog box appears.

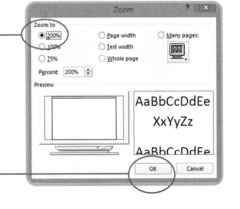

3 To make the document really big, select *200%* then click **OK**.

4 More options for how to view your document are available in the 'Zoom' Toolset.

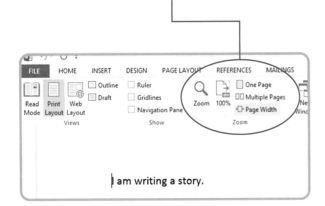

I am writing a story.

Top Tip!

Look at the 'Status Bar'. The 'Zoom Slider' is for quickly zooming in and out.

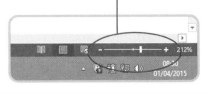

Read it like a book

Using **Read Mode** makes a document look like an e-book

If you want to read a document without all the Tabs, Toolsets and Buttons then try 'Read Mode'.

1 In the 'View' tab, click on **Read Mode**.

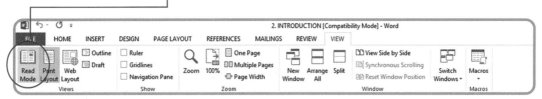

2 The document opens in 'Read Mode'. Click on the **arrow buttons** to change pages. Click on a picture to make it bigger.

3 You can also use your arrow keys on your keyboard, or use the **scroll bar** to change pages.

images: www.freeimages.co.uk

4 To change the color of the page go to **View**, then select a **Page Color** from the drop-down menu.

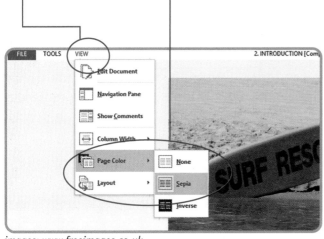

images: www.freeimages.co.uk

Top Tip!

You can switch between 'Read', 'Web' and 'Print' Modes on the 'Status Bar'.

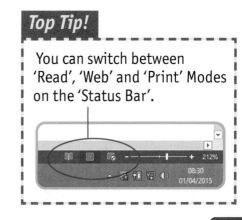

A head start

Using styled **Word** Templates

Word templates are a very quick way of creating many types of document for most of your needs.

1 Select the 'File' tab and go to **New** in the drop-down menu.

2 To find the type of template you want to use, type in the 'Browse field' and then click on the **Search icon**.

3 You can try 'Suggested searches' by clicking on a **Link** to a category.

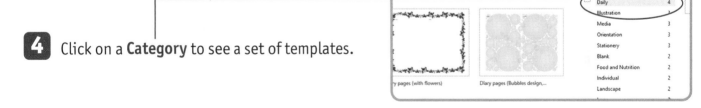

4 Click on a **Category** to see a set of templates.

5 Select the template you want. It will appear in a 'slideshow' window. Click **Create** to open the template.

You can start using the template straight away!

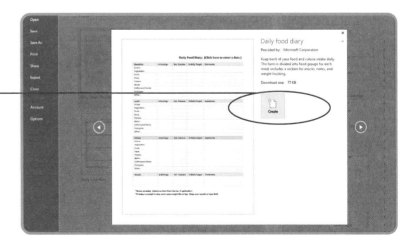

First steps project

Create a styled document

You will use skills learnt in this chapter to create your own invite.

1 Open **Word** and in the 'Browse field' type in *party invitation flyer*.

2 Select your favourite template and click **create** to make a new document.

3 Click and drag to **highlight** text you want to change.

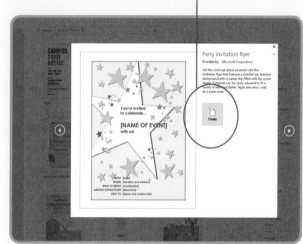

4 You can put in the date with the drop-down **calendar**.

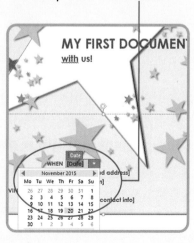

Top Tip!

In 'Read Mode' use the 'View' drop-down menu and select **Paper Layout**. This will allow you to view your document as it will print.

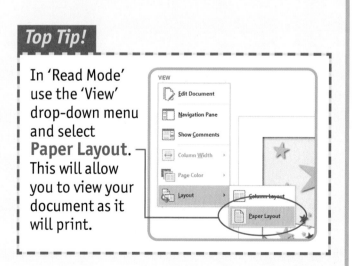

Font fun

From Arial to Wingdings3

One way to change how your document looks is to change the font. This is the letter style of text. Each font has a name, e.g. *Times New Roman*.

Top Tip!

Select some text in the document. Click the **Font** selector and hover-over a font name to see what your text will look like.

1 Open a new **Word** document.

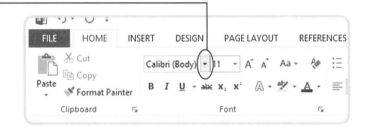

2 Click the **Font** drop-down menu.
A list of fonts appears.

3 Type and select some new text. Select a new **font**. Try *Arial Black*.

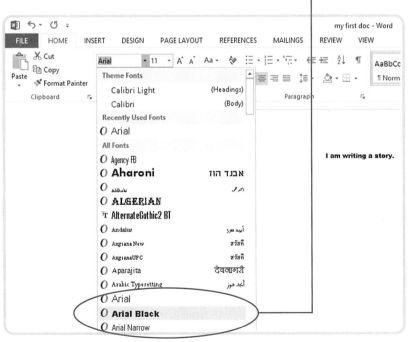

4 Type more text. Select it. Click the **Font** drop-down menu and try other fonts.

Size matters

Font sizes 1–72

Big letters make an impact. Small letters are harder to read but allow room for more information.

1 On the **Home** tab, click the **Grow Font** button. Start typing. Clicking the **Grow Font** button again makes the text even bigger.

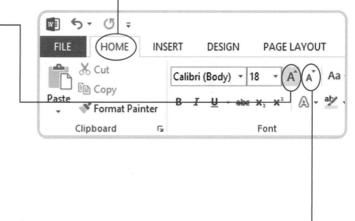

grow font bigger

2 Now shrink your text using the **Shrink Font** button.

shrink font really small

3 Select some text and choose a new size from the **Font Size** button drop-down menu. Hover-over a size to preview how it looks.

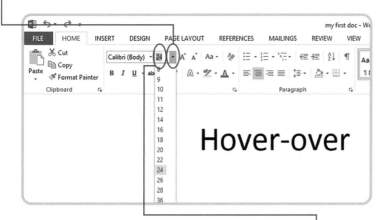

Hover-over

Top Tip!

Use the **Clear Formatting** button to go back to the font you had before

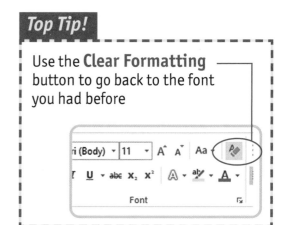

4 You can also type a size directly into the **Font Size** button field.

Getting on edge

Setting **Page Margins**

Changing 'Margins' helps your work fit on to a page.

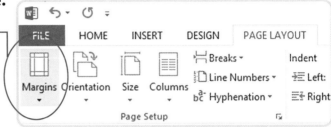

1 **Margins** are set from the 'Page Layout' tab or the 'Print Settings'.

2 There are several standard schemes.

3 If these do not suit, select **Custom Margins**.

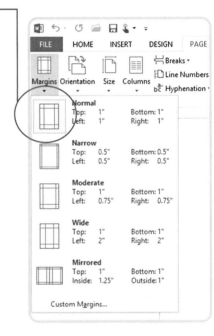

4 The 'Page Setup' dialog box allows you to set the margins exactly. Click the **Page Setup** drop-down. Type the margin sizes you want into the 'Margins' tab fields.

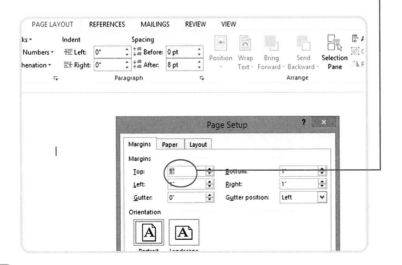

Top Tip!

Most printers can't print to the edge of the paper so don't make the margins too small.

Glee Club project

Create a flyer

Different fonts can be used for different purposes. Fonts can look serious, business-like, old-fashioned or fun.

1 Start a new **Word** document and save it as *Flyer 1* in a folder named *Glee Club*.

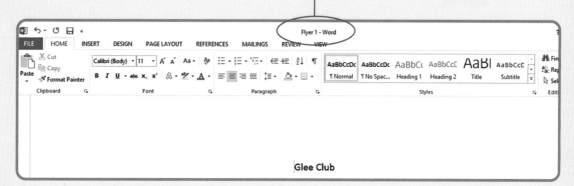

2 Type the heading *Glee Club*.

3 Add two blank lines and add some text about Glee Club.

4 Select the title and give it a *36* point font size and a fun font.

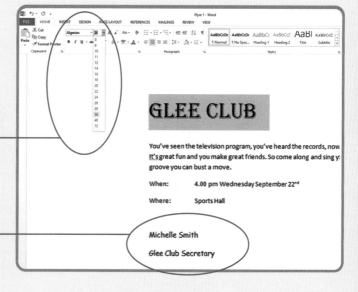

5 Press **Enter** twice and change the font to *Comic Sans MS*. Then type your name and your position. Make your name *16* point.

6 Set the margins to normal.

Creating text columns

Lay your work out in **columns**

Text columns make reading easier. Magazines are set in columns.

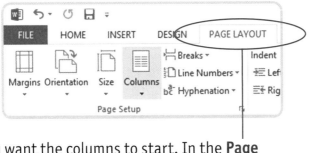

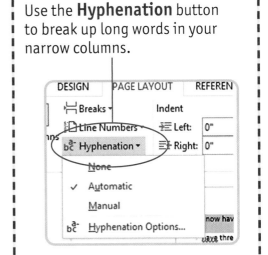

1 Click where you want the columns to start. In the **Page Layout** tab, click the **Columns** button drop-down menu.

2 Click on a standard column format, or select **More Columns** to define your own. The 'Columns dialog box' appears.

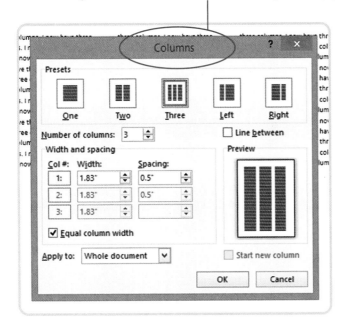

Top Tip!

Use the **Hyphenation** button to break up long words in your narrow columns.

3 Make your selection and click **OK**. Your text will now appear in columns.

Headers and footers

Give your pages a running head at the top or bottom

'Headers' and 'Footers' help keep your document together.

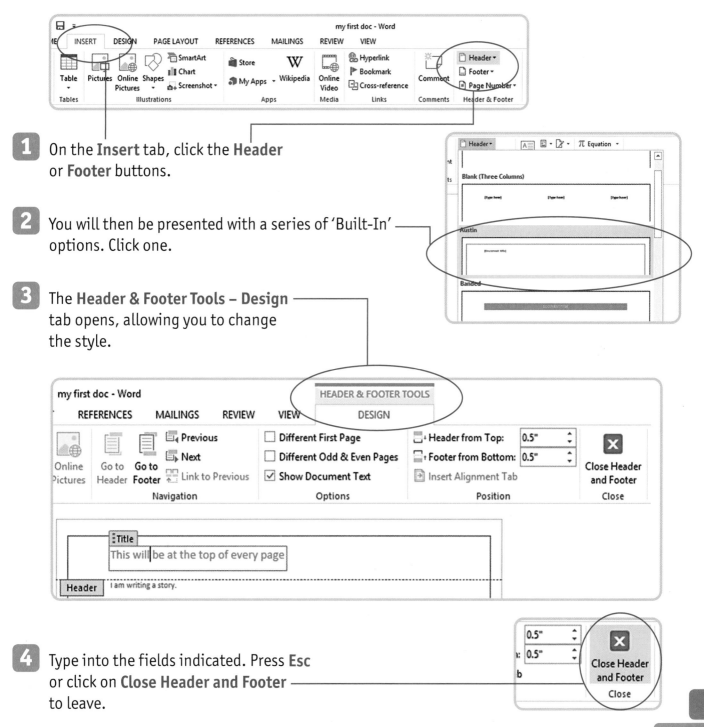

1 On the **Insert** tab, click the **Header** or **Footer** buttons.

2 You will then be presented with a series of 'Built-In' options. Click one.

3 The **Header & Footer Tools – Design** tab opens, allowing you to change the style.

4 Type into the fields indicated. Press **Esc** or click on **Close Header and Footer** to leave.

Page numbering

Page numbering helps keep your print-out in order

Page numbers help the reader know their position in a document.

1 From the **Insert** tab, click the **Page Number** button drop-down menu.

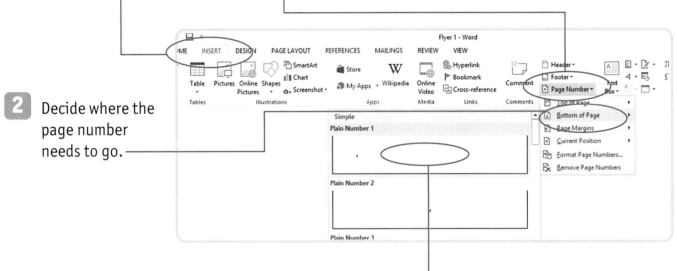

2 Decide where the page number needs to go.

3 Select a page number style from the list available.

4 A page number appears. Click-and-drag to select it. A floating **font toolset** appears. Use it to style the number.

> **Top Tip!**
>
> Double-click on the **Header** or **Footer** to change it again.

Glee Club project

Create a club news-sheet

You will use the skills you have learnt to set up a simple news-sheet.

1 Start a new **Word** document and save as *News sheet 1* in a folder named *Glee Club*.

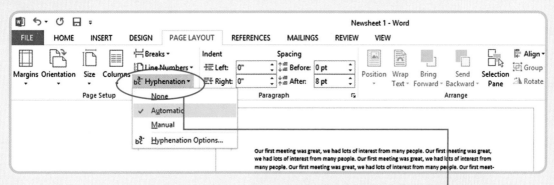

2 Type in lots of news and stories about your Glee Club. Set the **hyphenation** to *automatic*.

3 Set the columns to two.

4 Create a page header by typing in *Glee Club News*. Use an interesting font that's not too big.

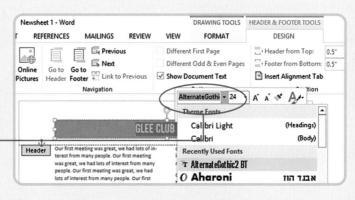

5 Create a page number. Change the height from the bottom of the page.

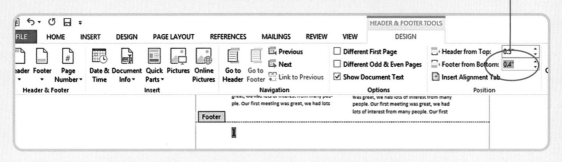

Time for a break

Page and Section Breaks

Adding 'Page Breaks' stops you worrying about pages shifting as you add text. 'Section Breaks' lets you change layout settings on the same page.

1 Click where you want to start the new page. ─────

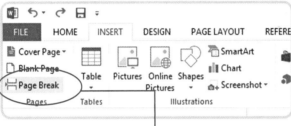

2 From the **Insert** tab, click the **Page Break** button. Create a chapter title at the top of the new page.

> ### Top Tip!
> The Keyboard command for page break is **Ctrl + Enter**.

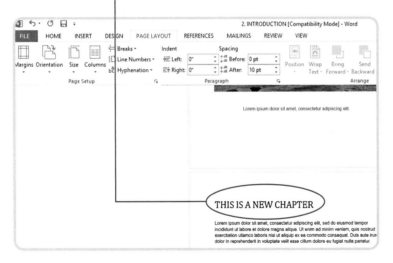

THIS IS A NEW CHAPTER

3 Click below the chapter title. For a 'Section break' on the same page, use the **Page Layout** tab and select **Breaks**. ─────

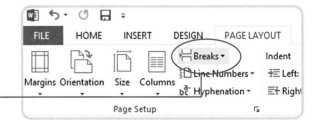

4 Select the **Continuous** option to start a new section on the same page.

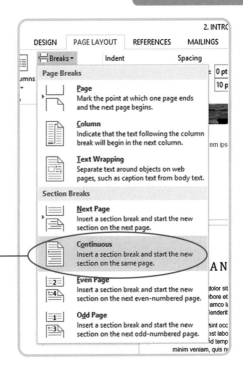

5 You can now set the text to **two columns** from the drop-down menu.

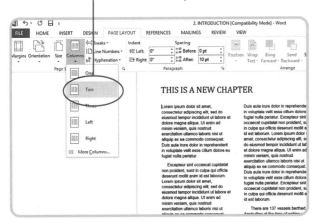

6 To rotate a page to landscape in your document, select **Next Page** from the 'Breaks' drop-down menu.

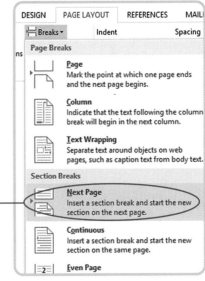

7 Select **Orientation** in the 'Page Layout' tab, then choose **Landscape**.

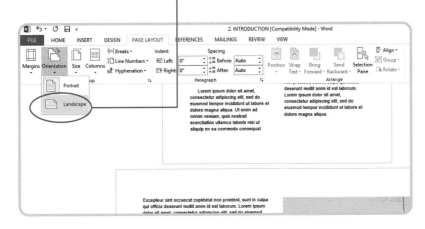

Left a bit, right a bit

Aligning paragraphs

Word automatically aligns lines of text to the left, but you may want the text to appear on the right or in the middle of the page.

1 Select some text. On the **Home** tab in the 'Paragraph' toolset, click the **Center** button. The line moves to the center of the page.

FILE	HOME	INSERT	DESIGN	PAGE LAYOUT	REFERENCES	MAILINGS	REVIEW	VIEW

Calibri (Body) | 11 | A˄ A˅ | Aa

Paste | Cut | Copy | Format Painter | B *I* U ▾ abc x₂ x²

Clipboard | Font | Paragraph | Styles

AaBbCcDc ¶Normal AaBbCcDc ¶No Spac... AaBbCc Heading 1 AaBbCcD Heading 2

Left aligned

Center

Right

This is justified text. This is justified text. This is justified text. This is justified text. This is justified text. This is justified text. This is justified text. This is justified text. This is justified text. This is justified text. This is justified text. This is justified text. This is justified text. This is justified text. This is justified text. This is justified text. This

2 Click the **Align Text Right** button. The line moves to the right edge.

3 Click the **Justify** button. Text spreads to touch both edges of the page.

4 Click the **Align Text Left** button. The text goes back to the left.

Glee Club project

Smarten your news sheet

Add a heading for your news story using 'Section Break' and 'Column' tools.

heading

Our first meeting was great
terest from many people. (
was great, we had lots of in
people. Our first meeting w
lots of interest from many

1 Open *News sheet 1*. Add *heading,* then put in a **Section Break** just after it.

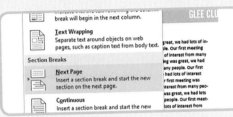

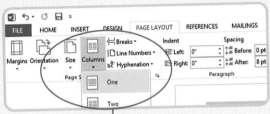

2 Click on *heading* and change it to **One Column**. Style the heading with the 'font toolset'. Click **Center** and type in your heading.

3 Highlight all the text on the page and select the **Justify** button to tidy up the columns.

White space

Use Line Spacing and Indents

You can change the look of your document by increasing space between lines of text or changing where text starts on a line.

1 From the 'Paragraph' toolset on the **Home** tab, click the **Line Spacing** button drop-down menu.

2 Select **1.5**. The space between lines of text becomes one-and-a-half times as big.

3 Select **2.0**. The space between lines is now double normal size.

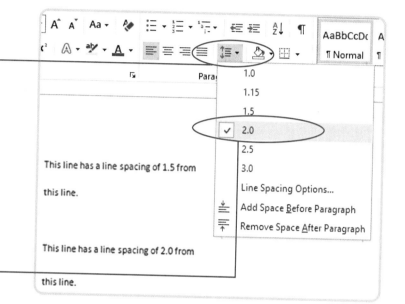

4 Select **Add Space Before Paragraph**, for more space, or **Remove Space After Paragraph** to remove it.

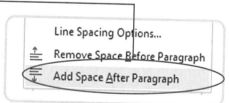

5 Click the **Increase Indent** button to start the paragraph further into the page.

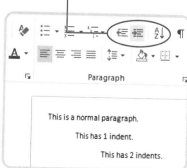

Top Tip!

Click the 'Paragraph' toolset drop-down menu to explore more options.

Add some color

Change the **color** of your text

Word can create really colorful work.

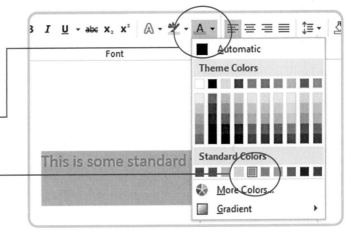

1 Select some text. From the 'Font' toolset on the **Home** tab, click the **Font Color** button drop-down menu.

2 Select a green from the 'Standard Colors' section.

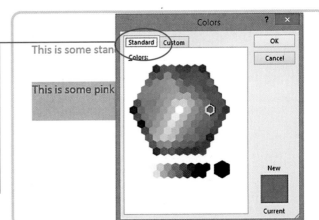

3 Now select *More Colors*. The 'Colors' dialog box opens. Choose a pink from the **Standard** tab. Click **OK**.

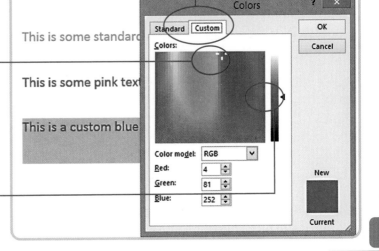

4 For more control, click the **Custom** tab.

5 Click in the 'Colors' area to choose a color. Click-and-drag on the 'Brightness Bar' handle to lighten or darken the color.

Be bold

Text styles: Bold, Italics, Underline and Strikethrough

Text styles are another way of making text interesting and emphasizing parts of your document.

1 From the 'Font' toolset on the **Home** tab, click the **Bold** button.

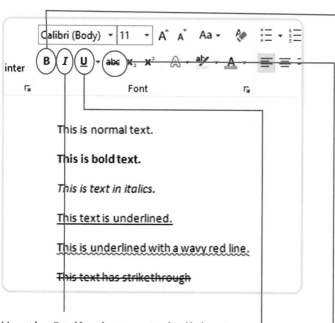

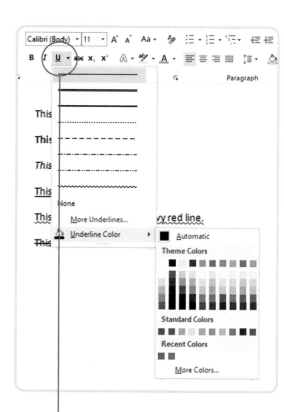

2 Use the **Italics** button to italicize text.

3 Click on the **Underline** button to underline text.

4 Using the **Strikethrough** button crosses out your text.

Top Tip!

You can mix all options, e.g. make text bold, italic and underlined.

5 Click the **Underline** button drop-down menu to see and use other underline styles.

Glee Club project

Liven up your flyer

Add color, styling and spacing to your flyer using what you have learnt in the last three pages.

1 Open *Flyer 1*. Add Indents using the **Increase Indent** button.

2 Create your own Glee Club color using the the **Custom** tab.

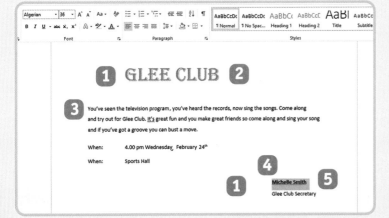

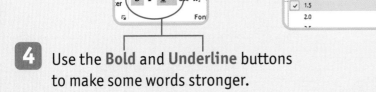

3 Space the lines out more using the **Line Spacing** button.

4 Use the **Bold** and **Underline** buttons to make some words stronger.

5 Use the **Underline** button to add a colored underline.

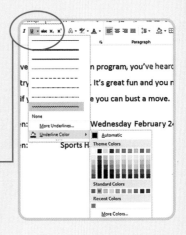

Now the highlights

Using the **Highlighter**

Highlighting attracts the reader's attention to important information.

1 The **Highlighter** button either highlights selected text or turns the mouse pointer into the highlighter pen.

2 When the mouse pointer has changed, click-and-drag it over the text you want to highlight.

3 To use a new color, click the **Highlighter** button drop-down menu and choose a new color.

4 To remove highlighting from text, select it and choose **No Color** from the **Highlighter** button drop-down menu.

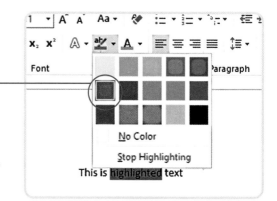

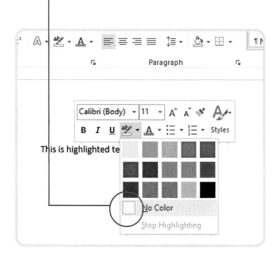

Top Tip!

Click the **Highlighter** button again to turn the highlighter off, or press the **Esc** key.

Paragraph emphasis

Style paragraphs using **Borders** and **Shading**

You can use paragraph shading and borders to color whole paragraphs in one go.

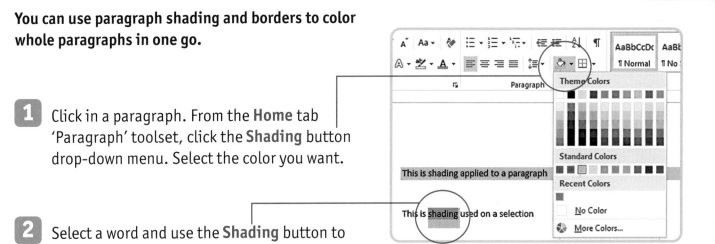

1 Click in a paragraph. From the **Home** tab 'Paragraph' toolset, click the **Shading** button drop-down menu. Select the color you want.

2 Select a word and use the **Shading** button to change its background color.

3 To add plain borders, click into a paragraph and then click the **Border** button drop-down menu.

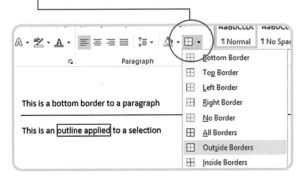

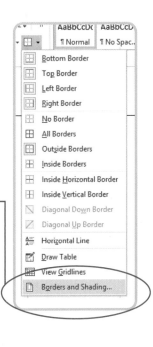

4 To add other borders, click the **Border** button drop-down menu and select **Borders and Shading**.

5 The 'Borders and Shading' dialog box appears, giving you more choices.

Consistent styles

Styles are combinations of font styling that help to keep the look of your document consistent.

1 Select a paragraph. From the **Home** tab 'Styles' toolset, click the **Title** style. The paragraph style changes.

2 Select some text and another style from the drop-down menu. That **style** is applied to the selected text.

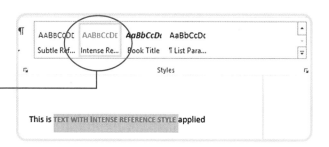

3 To change a style, right-click on it and select **Modify**. A dialog box appears.

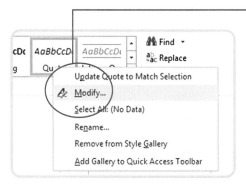

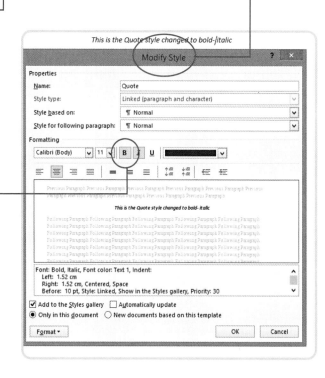

4 Change the font styling. Here **bold** is added. The paragraph style will change wherever it is used in the document.

Glee Club project

A new Glee Club style for the flyer

The 'Styles' built into Word won't always be what you want.

1 Select some text. Change the 'Font' and 'Paragraph' settings.

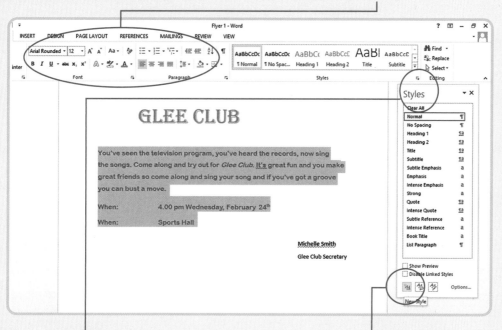

2 Click the **Styles** drop-down menu. Then click the **New Styles** button. A dialog box appears.

3 Name the new style *Glee Club text*. Click **OK**. This now appears in the 'Styles' drop-down menu and toolset.

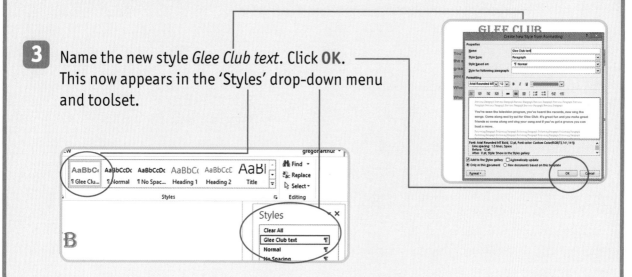

Outstanding text effects

Use WordArt in a document

'WordArt' allows colorful and exciting effects for your text.

1 Open *Flyer 1* or any document. From the **Insert** tab, click the **WordArt** button drop-down menu.

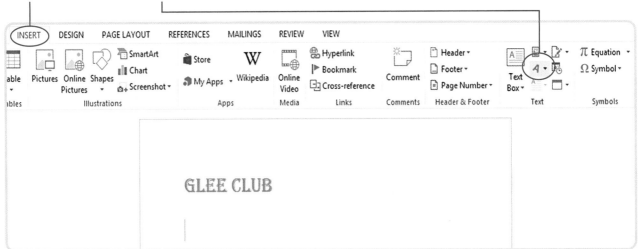

2 Select a **WordArt Style** from the drop-down menu.

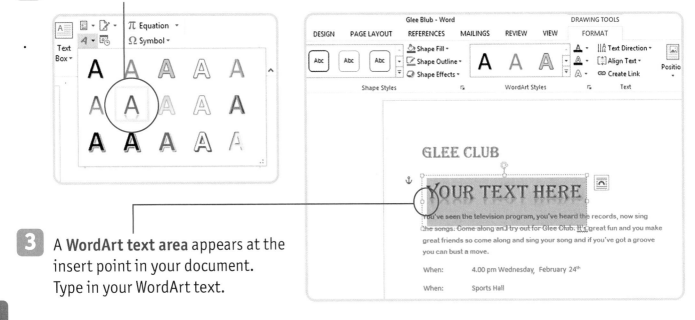

3 A **WordArt text area** appears at the insert point in your document. Type in your WordArt text.

4 The **Drawing Tools – Format** tab gives you formatting options.
Click on the **WordArt Styles** toolset drop-down menu.

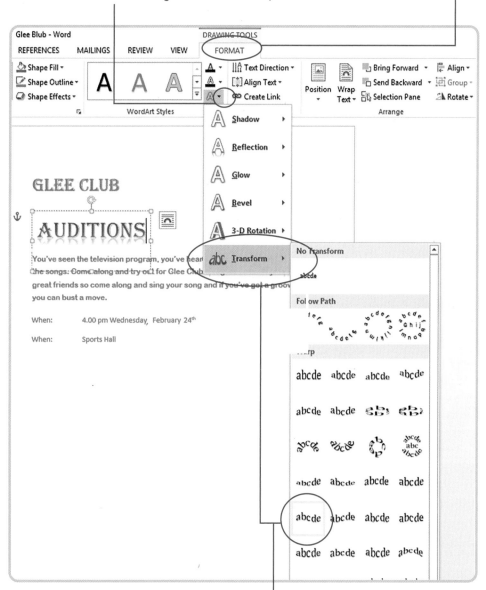

5 Modify the style using the options
in the **WordArt Styles** toolset drop-down menus.

6 **Word** can make your text look amazing. Try other
combinations of **WordArt Styles**.

Adding pictures

Add photographs and other Pictures

Top Tip!

Use the **View** button on the 'Insert Picture' dialog box.

Change your view.

With digital cameras and the Internet it's easy to put pictures into a document.

1 Click where you want a picture to go.

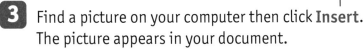

2 From the **Insert** tab, click the **Pictures** button. The 'Insert Picture' dialog box appears.

3 Find a picture on your computer then click **Insert**. The picture appears in your document.

4 Click-and-drag the **corners** to change the size of your picture. Click-and-drag the **rotate handle** to rotate it.

Playing with pictures

Changing **Pictures** after you have added them

The Picture Tools – Format tab has lots of options for styling your picture. Click on the picture to see this tool.

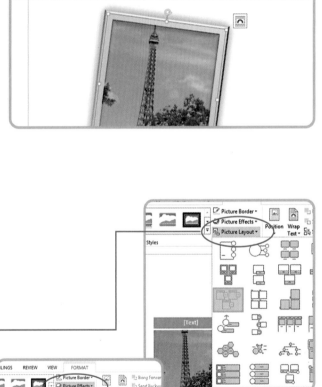

1 To add a border, select a border from the 'Picture Styles' toolset.

2 Change a frame color with the **Picture Border** button.

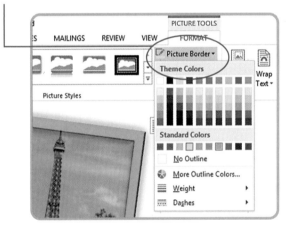

3 The **Picture Layout** button allows you to organize your pictures with captions.

4 The **Picture Effects** button adds cool effects.

41

Using Clip Art

Word can insert cartoons for you

Clip Art is pictures Word can use. There are libraries of Clip Art on the Internet.

Top Tip!

If you use a button like **Online Pictures** a lot, right-click on it and then click on **Add to Quick Access Toolbar**.

SmartArt | Store | W

Add to Quick Access Toolbar

1 Click into the document where you want the Clip Art to go.

2 From the Insert tab 'Illustrations' toolset, click the Online Pictures button.

DESIGN   PAGE LAYOUT   REFEREN

SmartArt
Chart
ctures Online Shapes
        Pictures   Screenshot
Illustrations

3 The 'Online Pictures' dialog box opens.
Type the name of the Clip Art you want in the Bing Image Search field. Then click the browse icon.

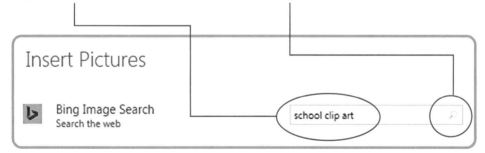

Insert Pictures

Bing Image Search
Search the web

school clip art

4 Information about the name, size and source of the picture appears in the bottom left when the cursor is over the picture.

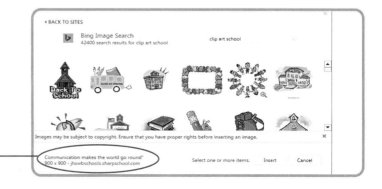

School fair poster project

Insert some Clip Art

Create a document called _Poster_. Use Clip Art to brighten up your poster.

1 Click on the poster where you want the Clip Art to go.

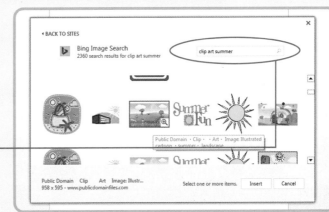

2 Search for Clip Art related to your school fair.

3 To select a Clip Art picture, click on it. Click on the **Zoom** icon on the bottom right corner of the picture box to see a bigger version.

4 To use the **Clip Art** picture, click on it. Then Click on **Insert**.

Clip an image

Using the **Screenshot** button

Word has a tool for capturing an image from a different window your computer screen.

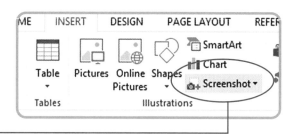

1 From the **Insert** tab, **Illustrations** tool-set, click on the **Screenshot** tool.

2 Select the **Window** you want from the new drop-down menu and an image of it will appear on your document.

3 Select the **Screen Clipping** tool from the drop-down menu if you only want to capture part of the screen.

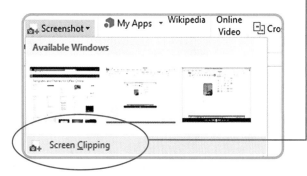

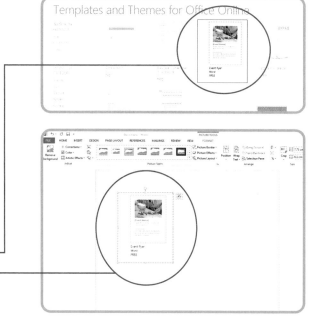

4 The window you want appears dimmed on full screen. Click-and-drag the mouse over the part you want and it will appear on your document.

Inserting shapes

Arrows, other **Shapes** and speech bubbles

Word has lots of shapes you can use.

1 Click the **Shapes** button.

2 Select the shape you want to use.

3 Click-and-drag the shape to where you want it.

4 The **Drawing Tools – Format** tab opens on the Ribbon with lots of extra features. Try **Shape Fill** and **Shape Effects** to change color and make your shape 3D.

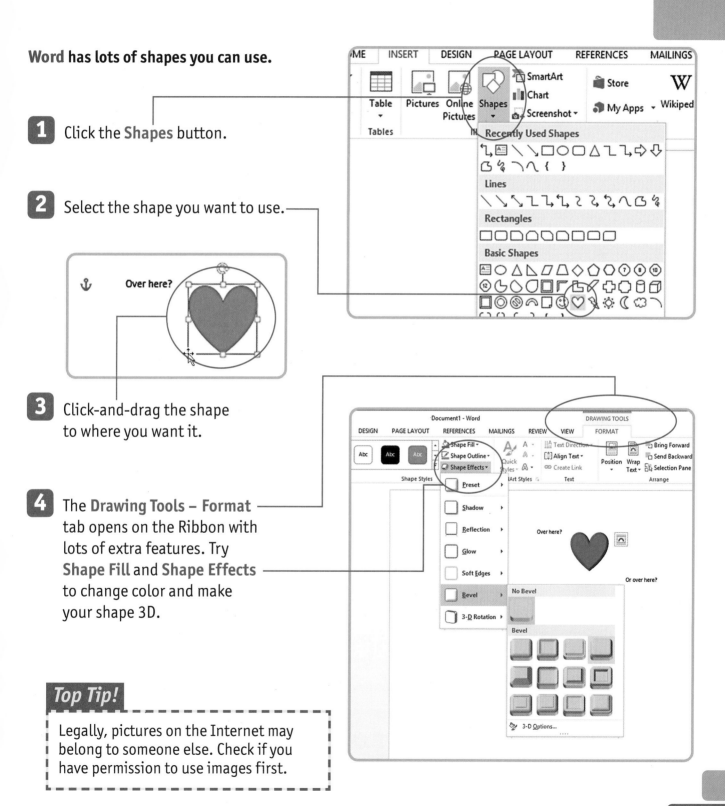

Top Tip!

Legally, pictures on the Internet may belong to someone else. Check if you have permission to use images first.

Text boxes

Add a block of text that you can move around

'Text Boxes' are a smart and fast way of adding text in many styles and layouts.

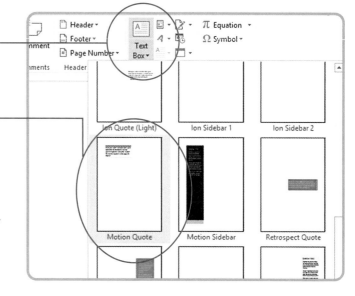

1 From the **Insert** tab, click the **Text Box** button drop-down menu. Select a text box style.

2 Click into the new text box and type your text. Click-and-drag the text box to move it, or click on the corners to change the size.

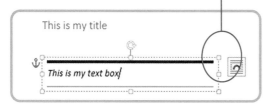

This is my title

This is my text box

3 The **Drawing Tools – Format** tab opens so you can change the styling of the text box, here using **Shape Fill**.

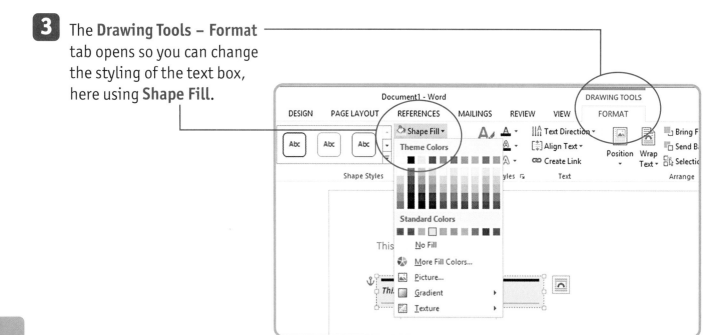

School fair poster project

Liven up your poster

Open your *Poster* document and add a fun heading style. Then add clips, shapes and text boxes to your poster.

1 Add a text box using the **Text Box** button. Style it with **Drawing Tools – Format**.

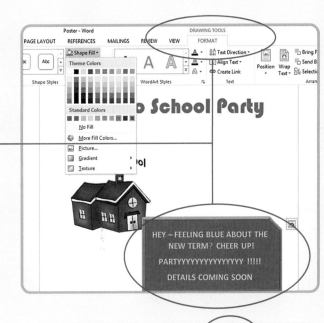

2 Click on the poster where you want a clipped image to go. Place it with the **Screenshot** tool and style.

3 Style the clip with **Drawing Tools – Format**, then use the **Shapes** button and style your shape with color and effects.

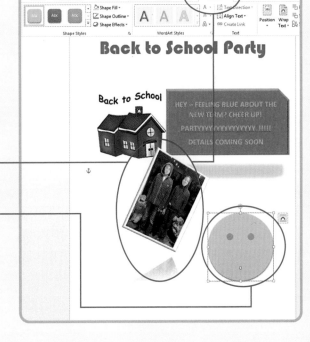

Working around graphics

Wrapping text around an object

'Wrapping' lets you fit shapes and images into text.

1 Click on the object you want to wrap text around.

2 From the **Format** tab, click the **Wrap Text** button drop-down menu.

3 Select a 'Wrap' option. The icons show you how the text wrap will look.

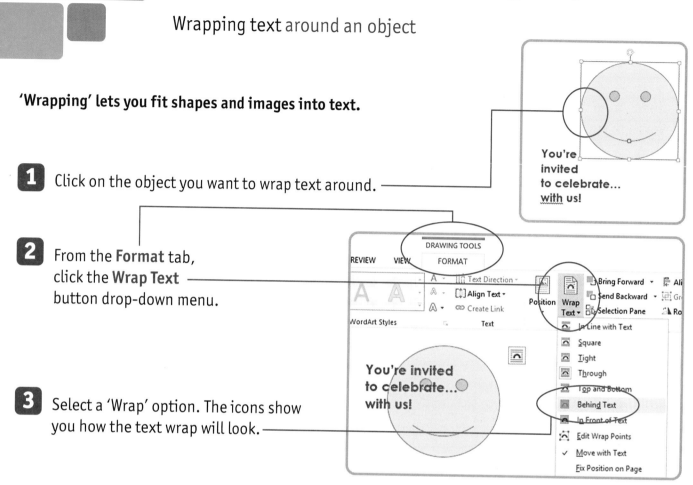

4 You can also use the **Position** button. **Word** has layouts for you to choose from with different image and text positions.

Background options

Change the background color or add a picture

You can add effects to the background of your document.

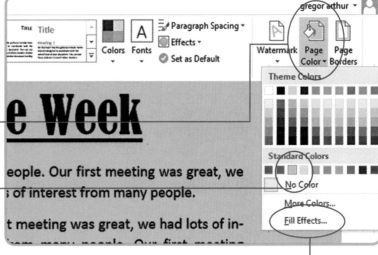

1 From the **Design** tab, select the **Page Color** button.

2 Select a background color.

3 To add effects or use a picture, select **Fill Effects**. The 'Fill Effects' dialog box appears.

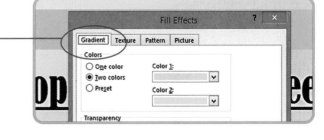

4 The **Gradient** tab effect changes the background color shades.

5 To have a background picture, click the **Picture** tab. To get the image you want, click the **Select Picture** button and choose a picture on your computer.

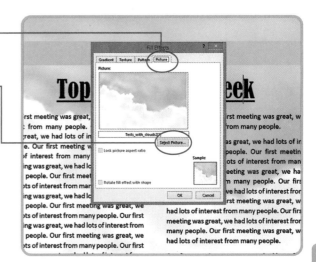

Border patrol

Adding Borders to your pages

A good border improves the look of some documents.

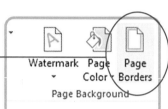

1 Click the **Page Borders** button on the **Design** tab. The 'Borders and Shading' dialog box appears.

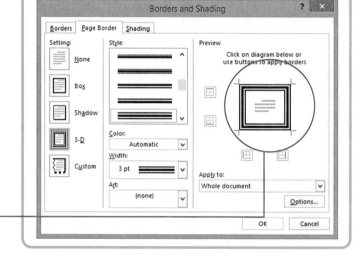

2 Set the 'Page Border', 'Style', 'Color' and 'Width' options. Check different combinations in the 'Preview' panel.

3 The 'Art' drop-down menu lets you make fancy borders.

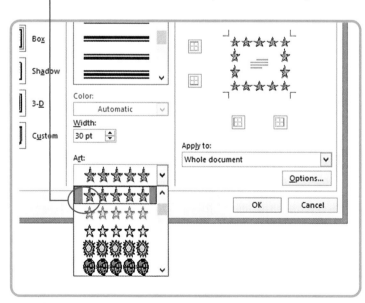

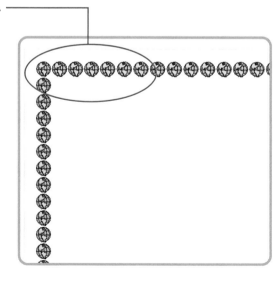

School fair poster project

Complete your Poster

To make it stand out on the wall, add 'wrap', a lively background and border.

1 Add some text and place over a shape using the **Wrap Text** button on the **Page Layout** tab.

2 Click on **Page Color** in the **Design** tab, then **Fill effects**. Find a background that works with the title text – try using the **Texture** or **Pattern** tab.

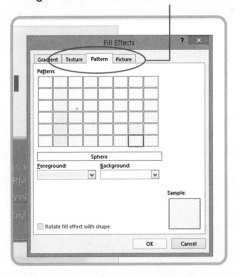

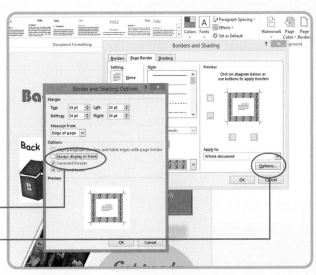

3 Add a crazy-looking border using the **Page Borders** tool. Try the **Options** button to allow a shape in front of the border.

Lively Layouts

Use Layout options and Align guides for fast layout

Layout options and Align guides let you see a clean and neat 'live' layout when you position items on the page.

1 Open *News sheet 1*. On the **Insert** tab, click the **Pictures** button.

2 The 'Insert Picture' dialog box appears. Select an image.

3 The image appears in the document with a **Layout Options** button floating next to it. Click the button to see the 'layout options'.

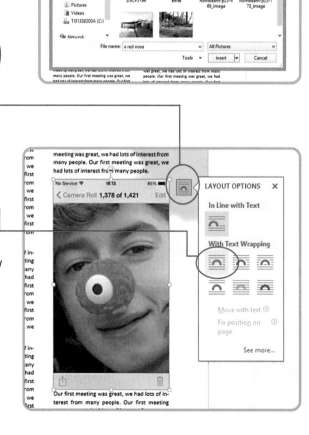

4 Select a **Text Wrapping** option. Now you can move the image around the page and the text will reflow at the same time around the image.

5 Place the image in the center of the page. To increase space around the picture, click on **See More** at the bottom of the **Layout Options** panel.

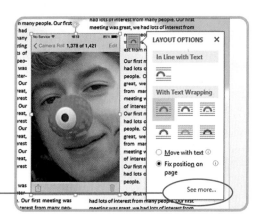

6 In the 'Layout' dialog box click on the **Text Wrapping** tab and change the 'Distance from text' values to *0.20 in*. You now see more space around the image.

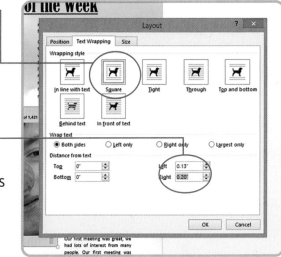

7 When you move an image or object, green guide lines sometimes appear. These help you align to the edges of other texts and objects. Your image will 'snap' into place when near a green **Align guide**.

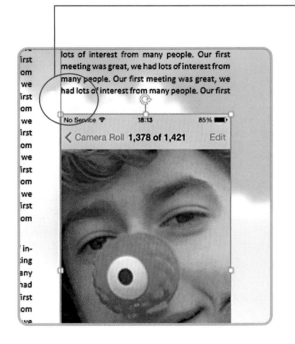

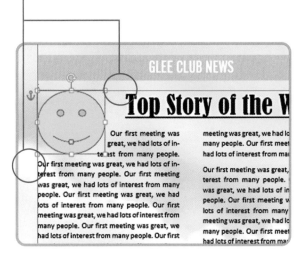

Easy design

Use **Themes** for easy document styling that can be changed with one click

Themes are sets of matching fonts and colors and effects. You can change your document very quickly with different themes.

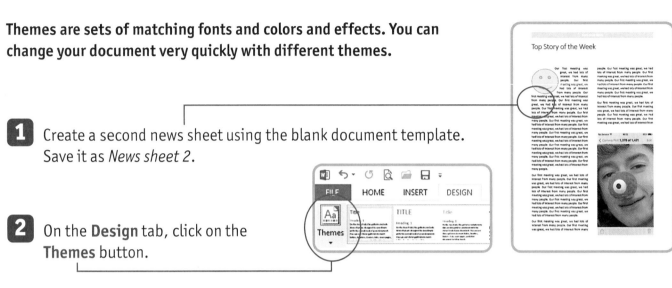

1 Create a second news sheet using the blank document template. Save it as *News sheet 2*.

2 On the **Design** tab, click on the **Themes** button.

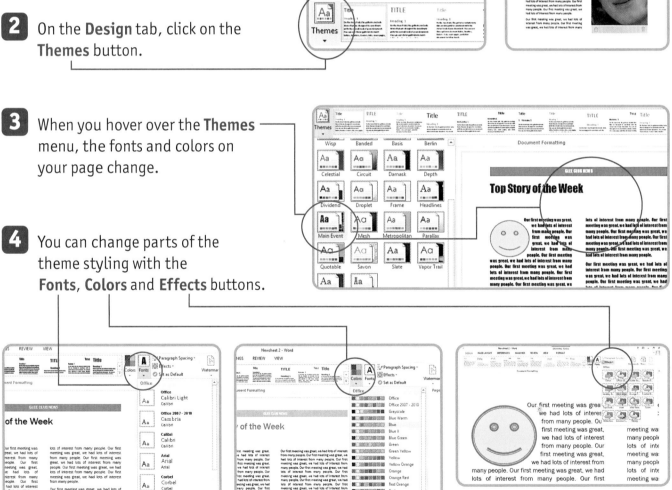

3 When you hover over the **Themes** menu, the fonts and colors on your page change.

4 You can change parts of the theme styling with the **Fonts**, **Colors** and **Effects** buttons.

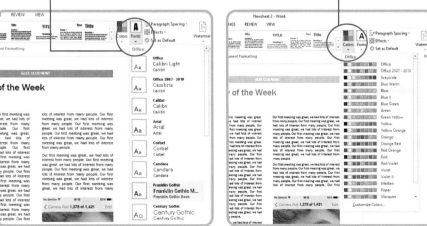

School fair poster project

Smarten your poster

Remove the old formatting and let Word do the styling work with themes.

1 Select the heading and click the **Clear all formatting** button on the **Home** tab.

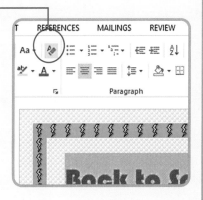

2 Change the heading to *Title* in the **Styles** menu.

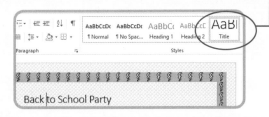

3 Press the **Themes** button and select a theme.

4 Make the title bigger with a different style.

5 Align the images better using **Align guides**.

6 Make changes with the **Fonts** or **Colors** button menus.

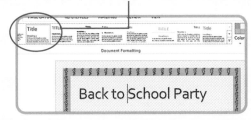

Be Smart

Use SmartArt for text in shapes that may be tricky for you

SmartArt is sets of shapes and text that you can use to communicate information clearly. Word creates the layout for you.

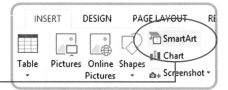

1 On the **Insert** tab, click the **SmartArt** button.

2 From the **SmartArt** dialog box menu, select an art style.

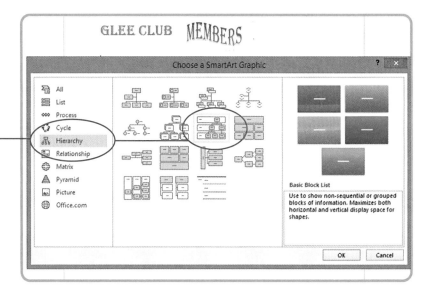

3 A 'SmartArt' appears on the page and the Ribbon changes. On the **SmartArt Tools – Design** tab, click **Change Colors**.

4 You can also change the style with the **SmartArt Styles** menu.

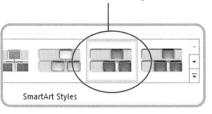

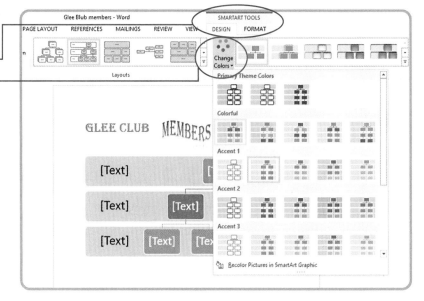

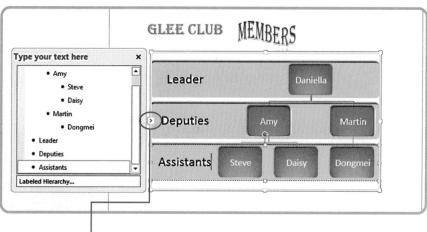

5 Click the **Text Pane** icon and a 'Text pane' appears. Begin typing into it. The text changes size by itself to fit in longer names.

6 To add a new shape, click an existing shape in the place you want it to go. Then click **Add Shape** and select its position from the menu.

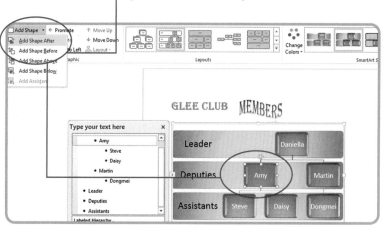

Top Tip!

Use the **Reset Graphic** button to undo your color and style choices.

7 A new shape appears. Use the **Promote** and **Demote** buttons to change the order.

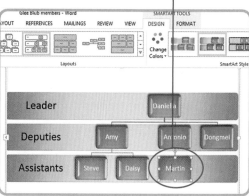

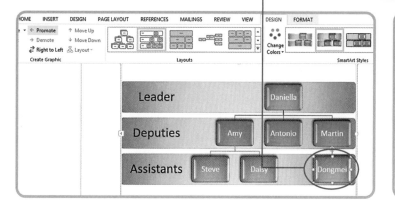

What will it look like?

Print Previewing your work

'Print Preview' gives you a good idea of what your work will look like when printed.

1 Click on the **File** tab and select the **Print** option.

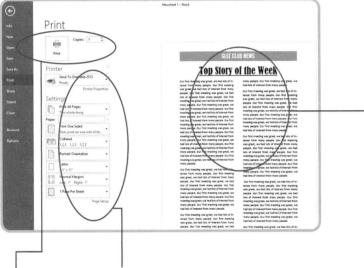

2 **Print** and **Print Settings** options are on the left. The **Print Preview** area is on the right.

3 The **Page Turner** area (bottom left of Print Preview) allows you to see each page.

4 Click the **Zoom to Page** button at the bottom right so you can see all of the current page.

5 Press **Esc** or click on to return to your document.

The long or the tall of it

Using different Orientations

Traditionally, a landscape painting is wide, while a portrait painting is tall. You can lay out your documents in the same way.

1 Go to the **Print** area and click on the **Portrait Orientation** button.

2 Choose from *Portrait Orientation* and *Landscape Orientation* on the drop-down menu.

3 The **Print Preview** will be updated automatically.

4 **Orientation** is also available on the **Page Layout** tab.

Print!

The **Print** button and other printing options

Simple printing is just a click away.

1 At the top of the 'Print Area' is the **Print** button.

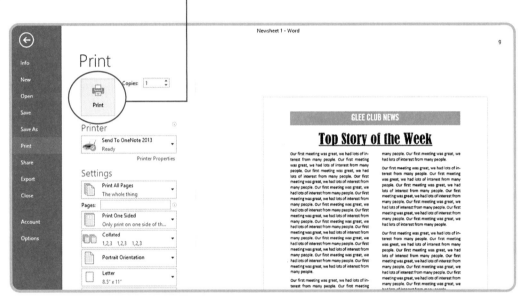

2 You can print off more than one copy by changing the number in the 'Copies' field.

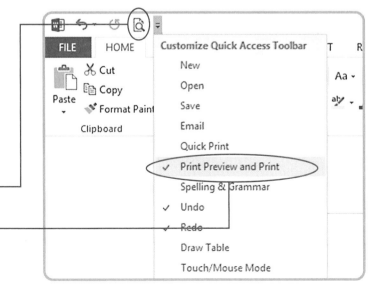

3 You can also use the **Quick Print** button in the 'Quick Access Toolbar'. To add a button to the **Quick Access Toolbar**, select it from the drop-down menu.

School poster project

Print your poster

Preview two versions of your poster, then print copies of the one you like best.

1 Open *Poster* and use the **Quick Print** button to open **Print Preview**.

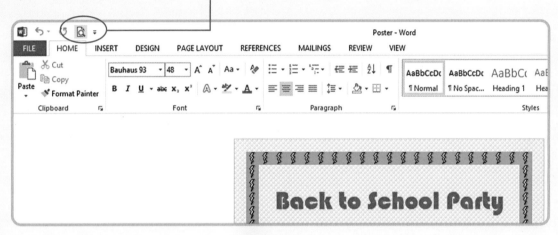

2 Go to the **Print** area and click
on **Portrait Orientation**.
Choose and view *Landscape*.

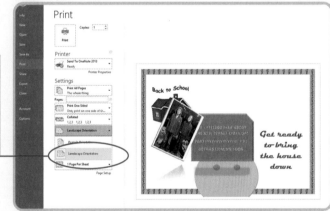

3 Choose the orientation you want
to use and increase the number
of copies to *5*. Then click **Print**.

Top Tip!

The position of shapes and
images can change when you
alter the orientation of your
document.

61

Go to web

Using **Web Layout**, **Hyperlink** and **Save As Web Page**

Not all work is for printing. Word allows you to make a simple web page.

1 Create a simple text file.
Click **Web Layout** in the **View** tab.

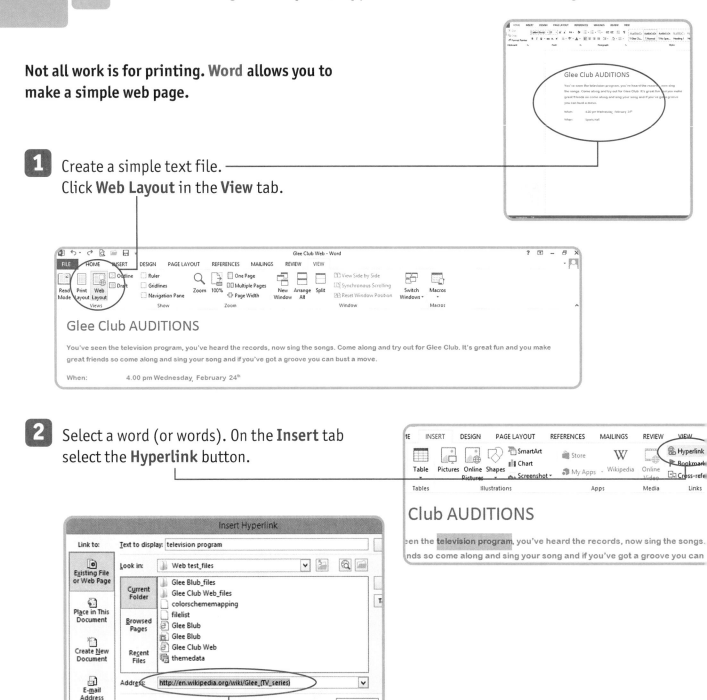

2 Select a word (or words). On the **Insert** tab select the **Hyperlink** button.

3 In the Hyperlink 'pop-up' box, type in the web address you want to link to. Click **OK**.

4 The words you linked are now blue with an underline. This shows they are linked to a website page.

5 In the 'Save As' dialog box select **Web Page** from the **Save as type** menu.

6 Open the web page in your web browser.

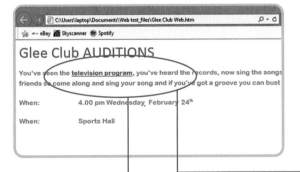

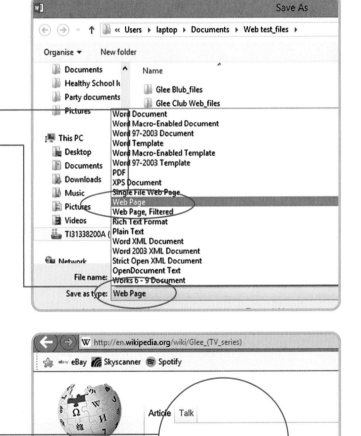

7 Click on the underlined text. The browser loads the website you linked to.

Bullet points

Using **Bullet points**

Bullet points make easy-to-read lists.

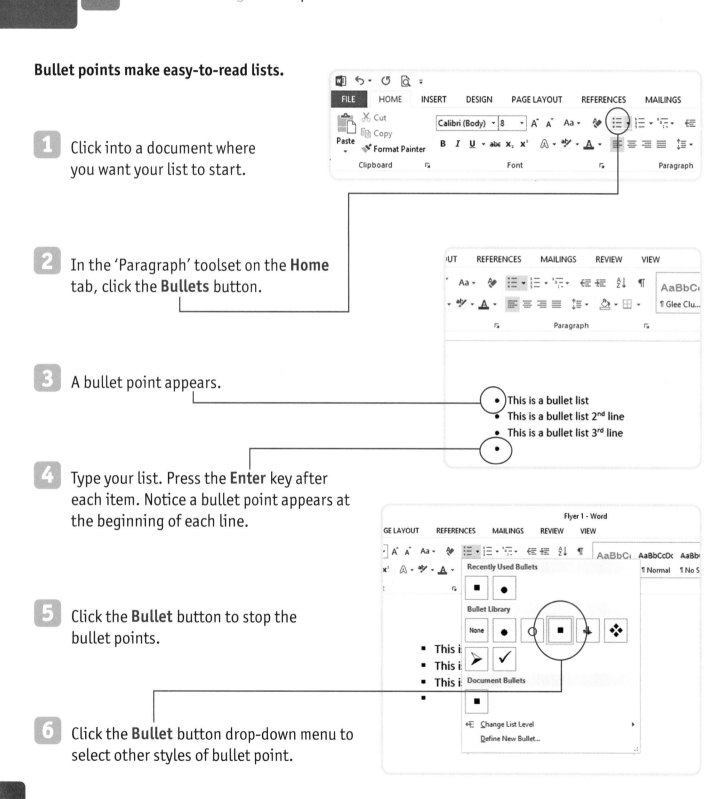

1 Click into a document where you want your list to start.

2 In the 'Paragraph' toolset on the **Home** tab, click the **Bullets** button.

3 A bullet point appears.

This is a bullet list
This is a bullet list 2nd line
This is a bullet list 3rd line

4 Type your list. Press the **Enter** key after each item. Notice a bullet point appears at the beginning of each line.

5 Click the **Bullet** button to stop the bullet points.

6 Click the **Bullet** button drop-down menu to select other styles of bullet point.

Numbered lists

Using a **Numbered** list

Bullet points make for easy reference, but numbered lists keep count as well.

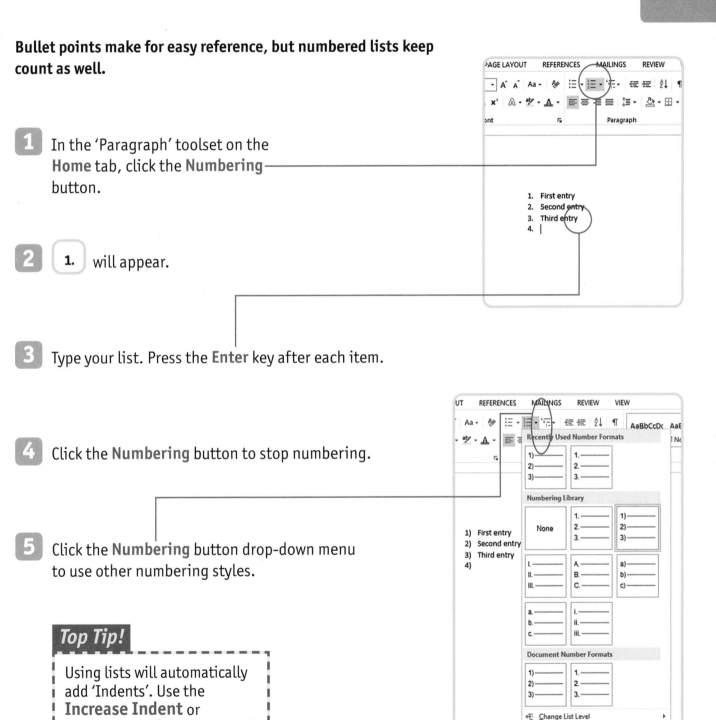

1 In the 'Paragraph' toolset on the **Home** tab, click the **Numbering** button.

2 `1.` will appear.

3 Type your list. Press the **Enter** key after each item.

4 Click the **Numbering** button to stop numbering.

5 Click the **Numbering** button drop-down menu to use other numbering styles.

Top Tip!

Using lists will automatically add 'Indents'. Use the **Increase Indent** or **Decrease Indent** buttons to change them.

Lists within lists

Using **Multilevel** Lists

It can help to break down your lists with more detail.

1 In the 'Paragraph' toolset on the **Home** tab, click the **Multilevel List** button drop-down menu.

2 Select a style from the 'List Library'.

3 Type a list. Press the **Tab** key to move a level <u>in</u> on the list.

4 Press **Shift** + **Tab** to move <u>out</u> a level.

5 List styles referring to 'Heading' need to be used with 'Heading' styles in the 'Styles' toolset.

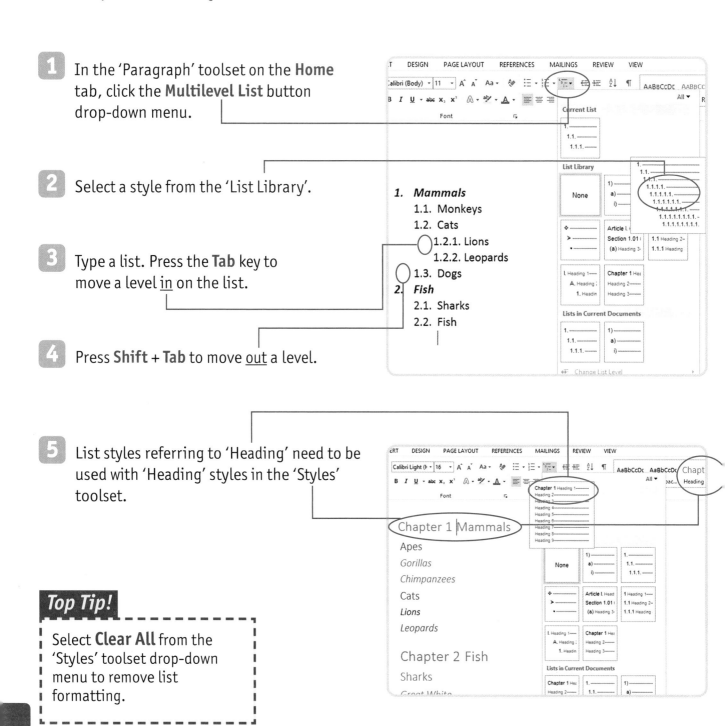

Top Tip!

Select **Clear All** from the 'Styles' toolset drop-down menu to remove list formatting.

Party planner project

Use lists to plan a party

Word documents are a great way to make lists.

1 Save a new document called *My Party* and subtitle it using different styles. Click the **Bullet** button and list what you need for your party.

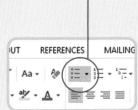

My Party

For my party I will need

- Guests
- Music
- Food
- Party games

2 Click the **Numbering** button. List the types of food you want.

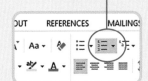

What food do I want?

1. Snacks
2. Savoury
3. Dessert

3 Change the numbering style to letters and list the drinks you will need.

What drinks do I want?

a) Fruit punch
b) Soda
c) Fruit juice
d) Tea & Coffee

4 Click the **Multilevel List** button drop-down menu and select a 'Numbered List' style. At the end of the first line press **Enter**, then **Tab**.

5 Add a type of snack, e.g. Chips and Dip. Click the **Enter** then **Tab** key to move in to the next level.

What food do I want?

1. Snacks
   1.1. Chips and Dip
      1.1.1. Salsa
      1.1.2. Guacamole
      1.1.3. Sour cream and chives
   1.2. Popcorn
      1.2.1. Toffee
      1.2.2. Butter
2. Savoury

Setting the table

Using **Tables** to lay out information

Word has great tools for quick, clear tables. You can choose from many different styles to save you time.

1 Click on your document where you would like a table to start.

2 From the **Insert** tab, click the **Table** button drop-down menu.

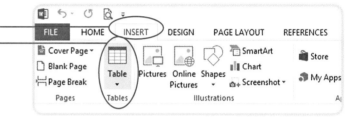

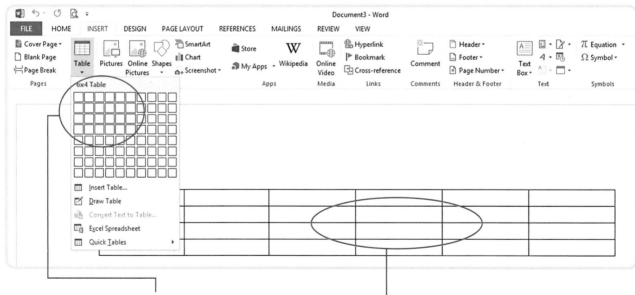

3 Select the number of rows and columns you want by click-and-dragging on the squares. This table has 6 columns and 4 rows. It appears in your document straight away.

Top Tip!

To add a new row, place the cursor in the bottom right-hand cell and press the **Tab** key.

4 The **Table Tools** tab set appears in the Ribbon.

5 On the **Design** tab, select a style for your table from the 'Table Styles' toolset.

6 Click on the 'Table Styles' library drop-down menu for more table styles. Hover-over table styles to preview.

7 Click into the table and start filling it in.

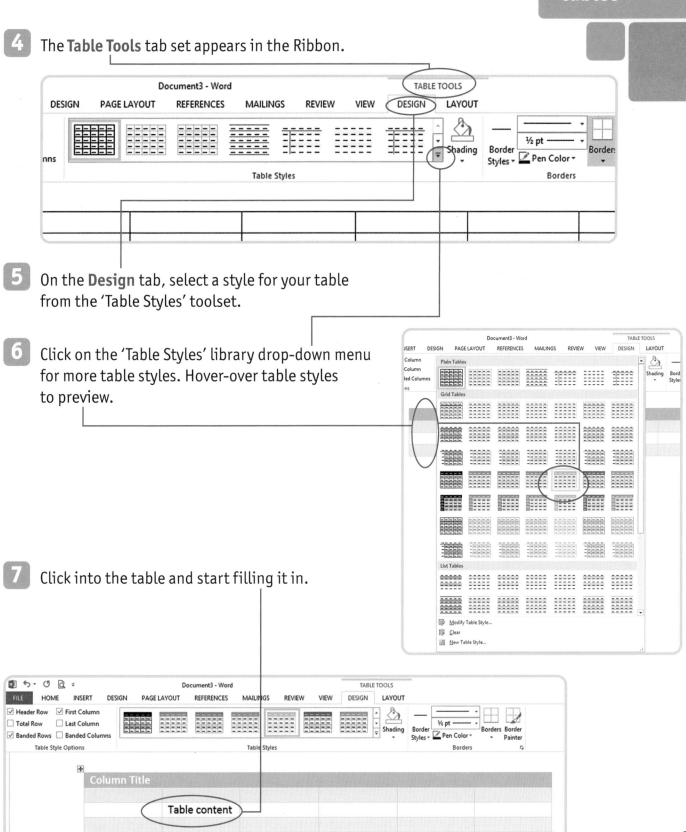

Table style

Table styles and options

The Table Tools – Design tab gives you options for changing your table.

1 In the **Design** tab, the 'Table Style Options' toolset allows you to change the formatting of table styles.

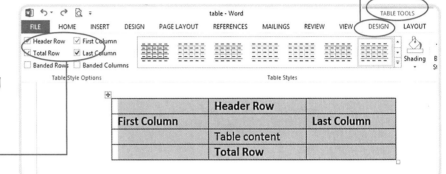

2 Setting the 'First Column' and 'Last Column' and 'Header Row' options adds emphasis.

3 The 'Banded' column and row options add color to alternate rows and columns.

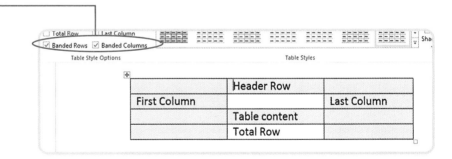

4 You can change the color and borders of cells using the **Shading** button drop-down menu.

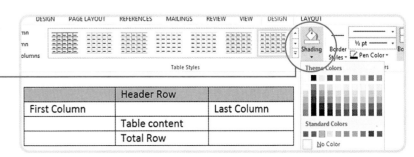

Party planner project

Create a checklist of party guests

Tables can be really useful. Where else would you put the party food? (Joke)

1 In a new document *My party checklist*, create a table with a row for each guest, a title row and five columns.

2 Click the 'Table Styles' library drop-down menu to see all styles. Hover and select a style.

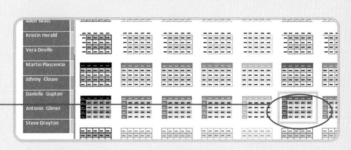

3 Make sure the 'Header Row', 'First Column' and 'Banded Rows' are the only options selected.

4 Select the *Dietary Requirements* column. Click the **Border Line Weight** button drop-down menu and set it to 3pt. Change the **Pen Color** to red and select 'Outside Borders' from the **Border** button drop-down menu.

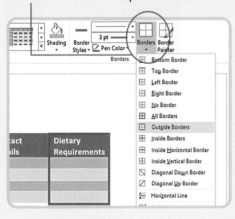

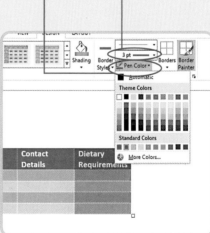

Table changes

Inserting, Deleting and AutoFitting rows and columns

Top Tip!

You can click-and-drag the columns in the ruler at the top of the screen to quickly change column width.

Tools for designing tables are on the Layout tab.

1 To add a row or column, click in the table where you want to add it. In the 'Rows & Columns' toolset on the **Layout** tab, click the appropriate **Insert** button.

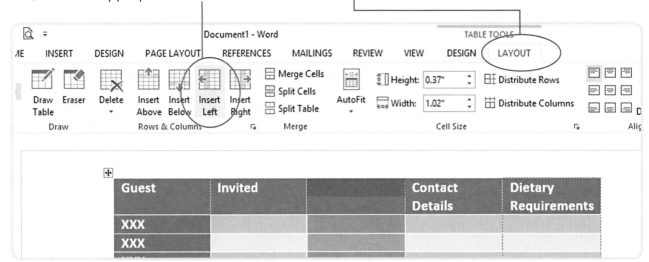

2 To delete a row or column, click on it then in the 'Rows & Columns' toolset click on the **Delete** button.

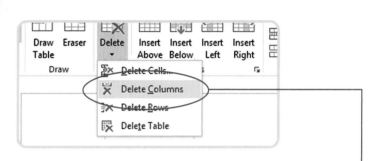

3 Select the delete option you need, e.g. **Delete Columns**.

4 To change a row or column size, select a cell within it. Then in the 'Cell Size' toolset on the **Layout** tab, increase the height of the row or width of the column.

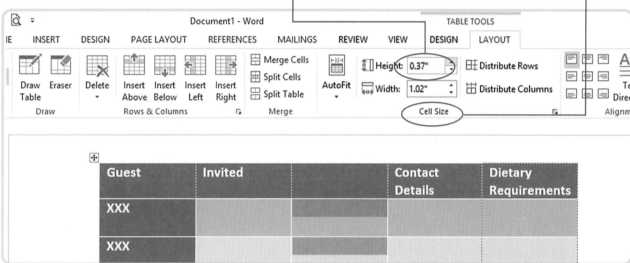

5 The **AutoFit Contents** option changes the column sizes to fit the text in each column. **AutoFit Window** adjusts the table to fit the page width.

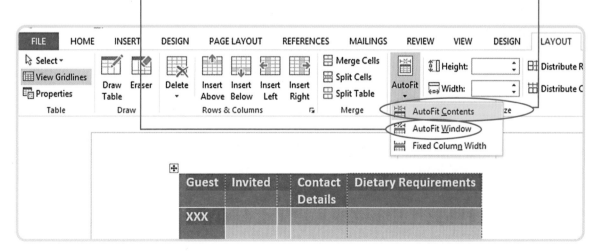

Other table tools

Merging, Splitting Cells and Text Direction

You can do many other things with tables. These options help you put the information in the right places.

1 To merge cells into one, select the cells then click the **Merge Cells** button in the 'Merge' toolset on the **Layout** tab.

2 To split cells after they have been merged or to add cells within a cell, use the **Split Cells** button.

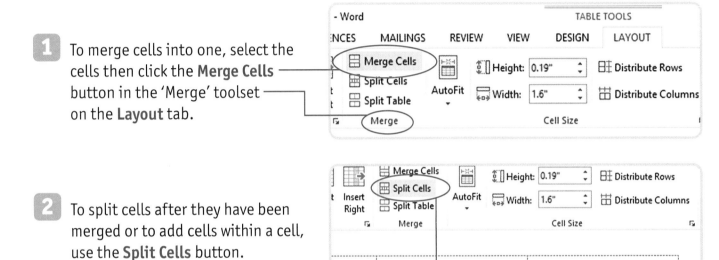

3 This gives you the option to choose how many columns and rows you split the cell into.

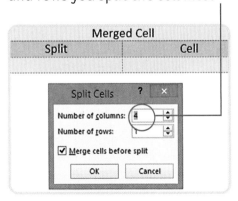

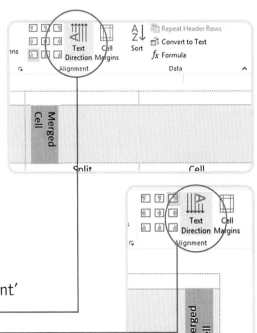

4 To change your text direction, in the **Layout** tab 'Alignment' toolset, click the **Text Direction** button. Click again to write from bottom to top.

Party planner project

Add some detail to your checklist

Using Layout tab options in your checklist.

1 Add a column to the left of the checklist.

2 Make the column narrower then merge the cells together.

3 Make the text direction bottom to top and type *Guests*. Center this in the cell.

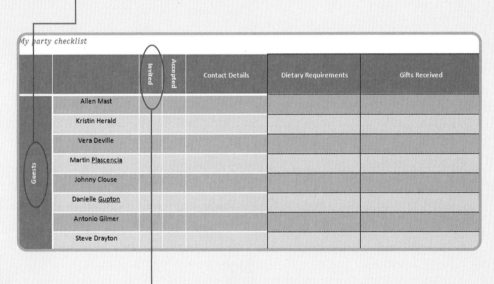

4 Make the text direction of *Invited* and *Accepted* top to bottom.

5 Make the *Invited* and *Accepted* columns very narrow.

Paint the table

Border Painter and Border Sampler

Colored borders between rows or columns are easy to make and draw elsewhere in a table using the Table Tools – Design tab 'Borders' toolset.

1 Create a table and then press the **Border Styles** menu button.

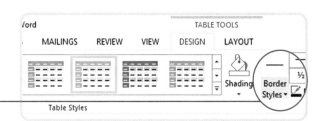

2 Select one of the **Theme Border** styles and color choices from the menu.

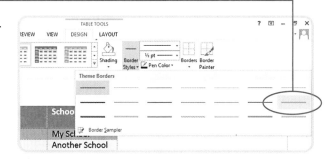

3 Increase the line thickness to *6 pt.*

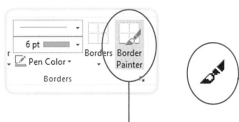

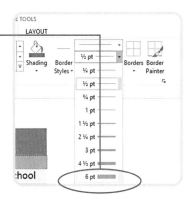

4 Press the **Border Painter** button.
The mouse pointer now looks like a pen.
When you click-and-drag between rows or columns it draws your border just like a pen.

Friend	Favourite Pet	Contact Details	School
Allen	Cat		My School
Martin	Cat		Another School
Farid	Cat		My School
Daniella	Cat		My School
Guang	Cat		Another School

5 Create another color border style using the **Border Styles** menu button.

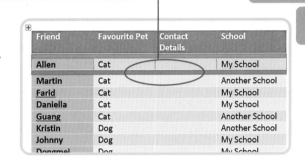

6 Save the document and close it. Open it again.

7 On the **Border Styles** menu, select the **Border Sampler** icon; the mouse pointer now looks like a pipette.

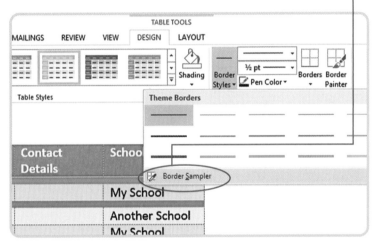

8 Move the pipette over a border you want to copy and click on it. The pipette will change to a pen. Draw the copied style anywhere on the table.

Friend	Favourite Pet	Contact Details	School
Allen	Cat		My School
Martin	Cat		Another School
Farid	Cat		My School
Daniella	Cat		My School
Guang	Cat		Another School
Kristin	Dog		Another School
Johnny	Dog		My School
Dongmei	Dog		My School
Steve	Dog		My School
Vera	Fish		Another School
Antonio	Fish		Another School
Akila	Fish		Another School

Table super-tools

The **Plus Sign** and **Table Eraser**

It's easy to add columns and rows, or rub out table cell borders using the Table Tools – Layout or Design tab tools that appear when you've clicked in a table.

1 To add more rows or columns, move the mouse pointer to the edge of a table; a **Plus Sign** appears.

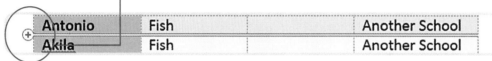

2 Click the **Plus Sign** once or more; extra rows will appear.

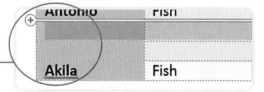

3 If you want parts of the table to look blank you can use the **Eraser** tool in the **Table Tools – Layout** tab.

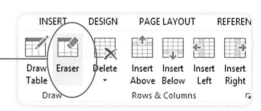

4 Click the **Eraser** button. The mouse pointer now looks like an eraser.

5 Click-and-drag over cells you don't want. A box appears to show what will be erased.

6 Cell borders and text are erased when the mouse button is released.

Party planner project

Some corrections for your checklist

Using Design tab options in your checklist.

1 Click the **Plus Sign** for an extra row of guests at the top.

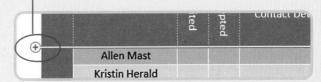

2 Click the **Border Styles** button to select the **Border Sampler**. Click in a Guest row.

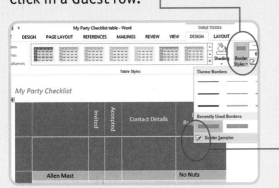 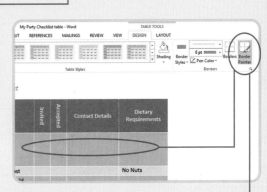

3 Press the **Border Painter** button. Click-and-drag across the new row. The row color changes to match the Guest row.

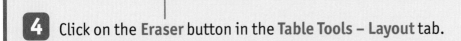

4 Click on the **Eraser** button in the **Table Tools – Layout** tab.

5 Delete the unwanted cell border. Tidy up the table.

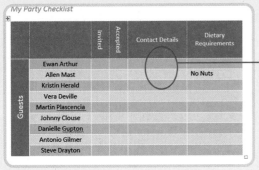

Turn back time

Using the Undo, Redo and Repeat buttons

It's easy to make a mistake and just as easy to correct it, even if correcting the mistake was a mistake!

1 Make a spelling mistake in a document.

2 From the 'Quick Access' toolbar, click the **Undo** button.

3 The mistake is corrected to what it was before. To undo more than one mistake, keep clicking the **Undo** button.

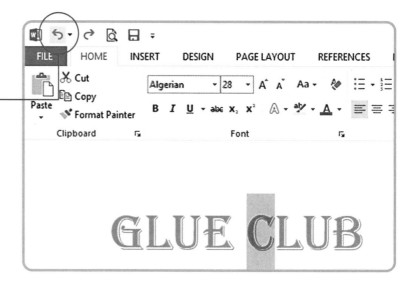

Top Tip!

The keyboard shortcut for 'Undo' is pressing the **Ctrl** + **Z** keys.

4 Or click the **Undo** button drop-down menu. A list of your recent actions appears. Click the action you want to undo.

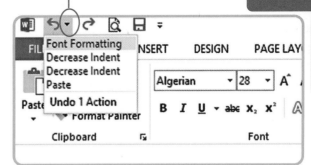

5 You can also undo more actions on the list by highlighting more than one at once.

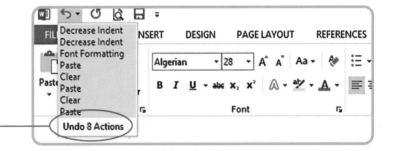

6 If you decide you don't want to undo something after all, click the **Redo** button. You can keep clicking this until you are back to where you started.

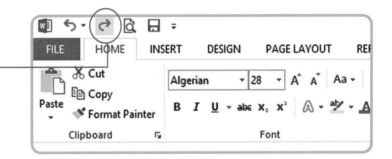

7 If you haven't undone anything the **Redo** button becomes the **Repeat button**; it repeats your last action.

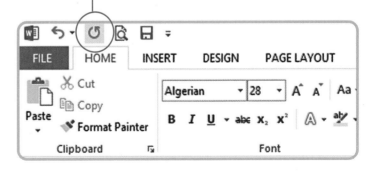

Copy and paste

Repeat something without having to retype it

Duplicating text is quicker than typing it again.

1 Select text you want to copy.

2 In the 'Clipboard' toolset on the **Home** tab select **Copy**.

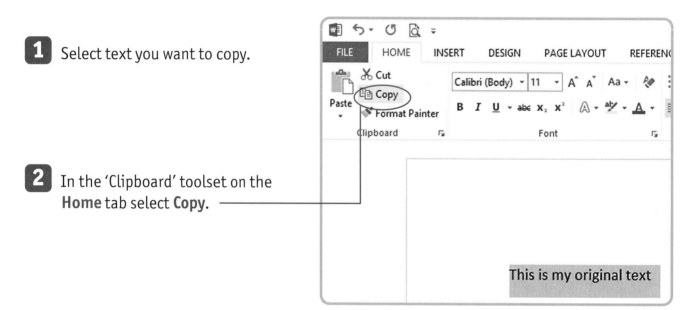

3 Move the cursor to where you want the copied text to go.

4 Click the **Paste** button.

5 The copied text appears.

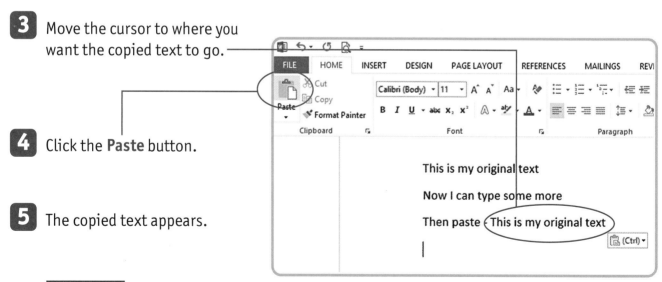

Top Tip!

You can 'Copy' and 'Paste' between **Word** and other programs.

Party invite project

Use copy, paste and undo to save time

Doing boring jobs can be quicker using Copy and Paste, and you can Undo if you make a mistake.

1 Name a document *List of friends*. Type the names of friends to invite to a party.

2 Create a *Party Invite* using the **Word** template shown.

3 Copy a name from your list and paste, using the cursor to select where you want the copied text to go.

4 To get the style of copied text to match the new style, use the paste options. Here the **Keep text only** button is selected. This stops the old style appearing.

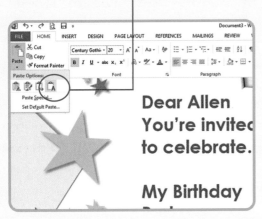

Moving

Move your work around

'Cut' and 'Paste' help you reorganize work.

1 Select the text that you want to move.

2 Click **Cut** from the 'Clipboard' toolset. The text disappears.

3 Click where you want the text to go.

4 Select **Paste**. The text reappears in the new position.

5 If the text is a different style at the new position, use the **Paste Options** drop-down menu that appears next to the pasted text and select **Merge Formatting**.

6 The pasted text is now the same style as the surrounding text.

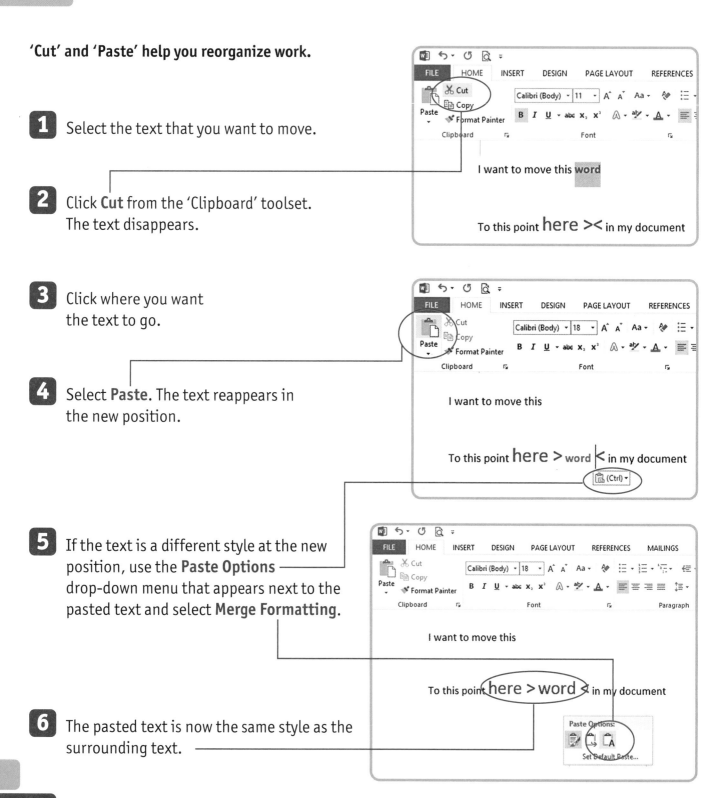

The history of clipping

Using the Clipboard

The 'Clipboard' allows you to reuse anything that you have copied in Microsoft Office and other compatible programs, not just Word.

1 Open the *List of friends* document and copy the names, one at a time. Then open *Party Invite*.

Steven
Antonio
Danielle
Farid
Akila
Quan
Bernard
Daisy
Dongmei

2 From the 'Clipboard' toolset on the **Home** tab, select the toolset drop-down menu.

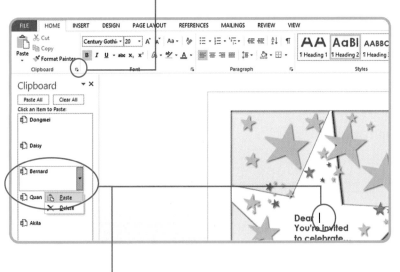

3 Place the cursor and then click on the 'clip' that you want to paste.

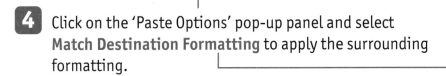

4 Click on the 'Paste Options' pop-up panel and select **Match Destination Formatting** to apply the surrounding formatting.

Repeat your style

Using the Format Painter

We have copied and pasted text. The 'Format Painter' copies styles.

1 In a document, click on text that has the format you want to copy.

2 Click the **Format Painter** button. The selected formatting is copied and the mouse pointer changes to a paintbrush.

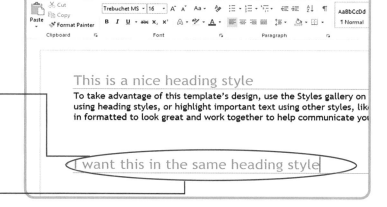

3 Move the 'Format Painter' over the text you want to copy the format to.

4 Click-and-drag over the text you want to change.

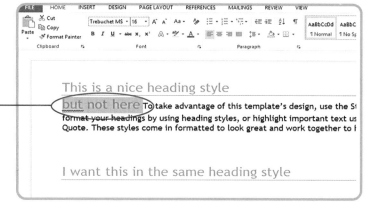

5 The 'Format Painter' works once only. Click the button again if you want to repeat using it. Press **Esc** if you don't want to use it after all.

Party thank you project

Use the clipboard to create lots of thank you letters

Once the names are on the clipboard, it's easy to create the thank you letters.

1 Open your party planning document. Select the name of each guest and copy it.

2 Create a new document called *Party thank you*. Then open the 'Clipboard' drop-down menu and type some content for your letter.

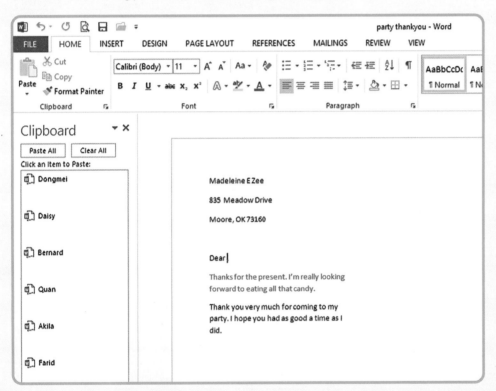

3 Delete the original name in your letter and paste a new name from the Clipboard.

4 Save the *Thank you* letter with a new file name. Reopen the original *Thank you* letter and repeat so you have a letter for each guest.

What's the time?

Inserting the Time or Date and
other Symbols

Word makes life easier with some quick tools.

1 Click where you want the date or time to go.

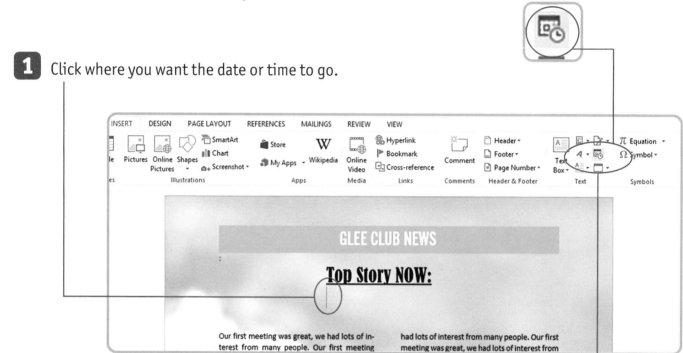

2 From the 'Text' toolset on the **Insert** tab, click the **Date & Time** button. The 'Date & Time' dialog box appears.

3 Select the format you need.

4 If you want the date or time to be the current one, tick 'Update automatically'.

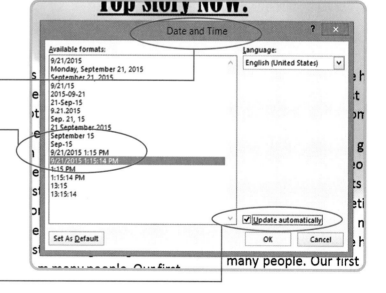

5 The date and time will update when you reopen the document, or you can click on it and then select the **Update** tab that appears.

6 Click the **Symbol** button drop-down menu on the **Insert** tab.

Your date and time format settings come from Window's 'Time and language' settings in 'PC Settings'.

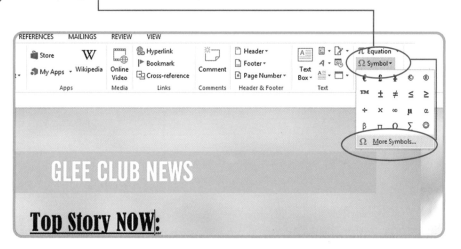

7 In the 'Symbol' dialog box that appears, change the font to 'Wingdings'. Select a clock icon and click **Insert**. It will appear in your text.

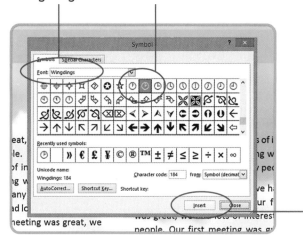

Finding other words

Using the Thesaurus

Word has a great tool for alternatives to words. How about *wonderful* **and** *fantastic* **as alternatives to** *terrific***.**

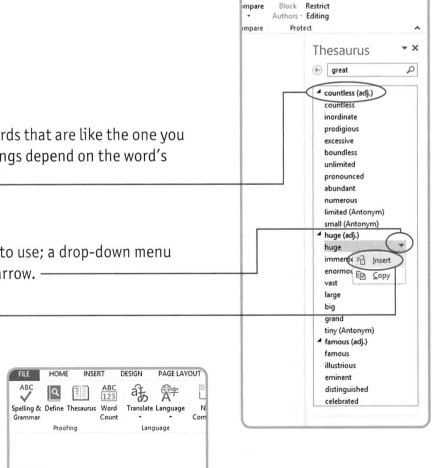

1 Click on the word you want another word for, like *great*.

2 On the **Review** tab, click the **Thesaurus** button in the 'Proofing' toolset.

3 The **Thesaurus** Pane appears.

4 The **Thesaurus** shows other words that are like the one you clicked on. The different headings depend on the word's meaning.

5 Hover-over the word you want to use; a drop-down menu appears. Click the drop-down arrow.

6 Select **Insert** to add that word to your document or **Copy** to use it later.

Party thank you project

Make your language more interesting

Make your *thank you* letter more interesting and learn about more words with the Thesaurus.

1 Open a *thank you* letter. Style with handwriting font *Bradley Hand ITC*.

2 Click on a common word like *good*.

3 Check the list of similar words.

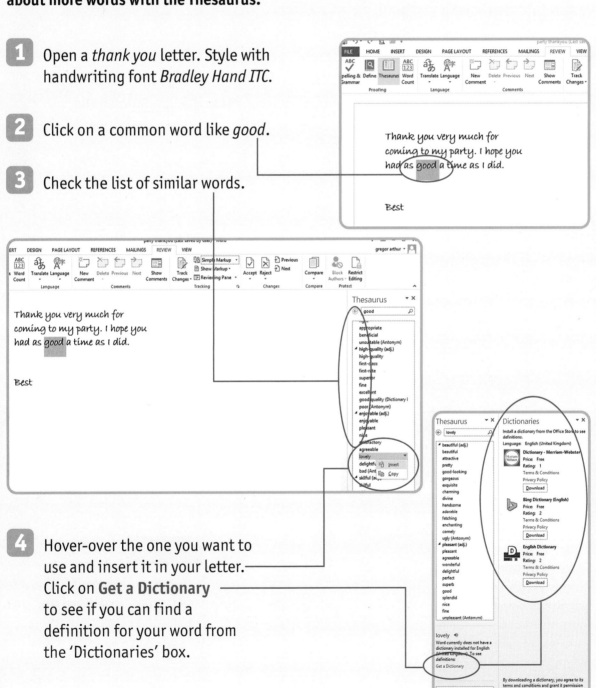

4 Hover-over the one you want to use and insert it in your letter. Click on **Get a Dictionary** to see if you can find a definition for your word from the 'Dictionaries' box.

Check the text

Using the Spell checker

Squiggly red or blue lines appear under some words to show that Word thinks they may contain a spelling or grammar mistake.

1 If a squiggly line appears under a word, right-click on it.

2 If it is a <u>red</u> line, this menu will appear.

3 Choose the right spelling from the possibilities. If the spellings are not what you want, select **Ignore All**. Select **Add to Dictionary** if you use this word often.

4 If it's a <u>blue</u> line then it's a grammar mistake. Right-click on it and **Word** will offer you what it thinks is right or tell you what it thinks is wrong.

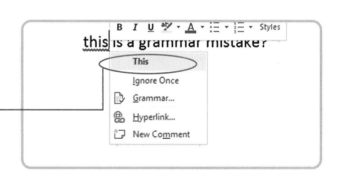

Top Tip!

'Grammar tips' can be hard to get rid of. Use **Word options** from the **File** tab to hide them. Click to remove the tick from the 'Check grammar with spelling' check box in the **Proofing** section.

5 To check a <u>whole</u> document, click the
Spelling & Grammar button in the **Review** tab.

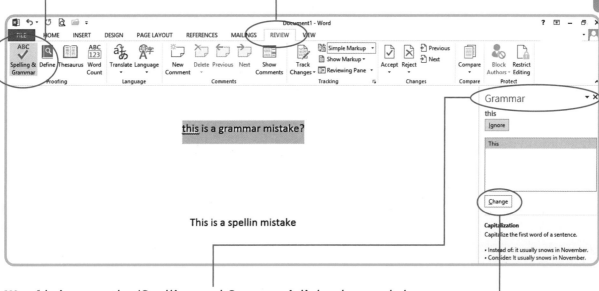

6 **Word** brings up the 'Spelling and Grammar' dialog box and shows each query one at a time.

7 You can choose from the suggestions and **Change** or **Ignore**.
It will then go on to the next one.

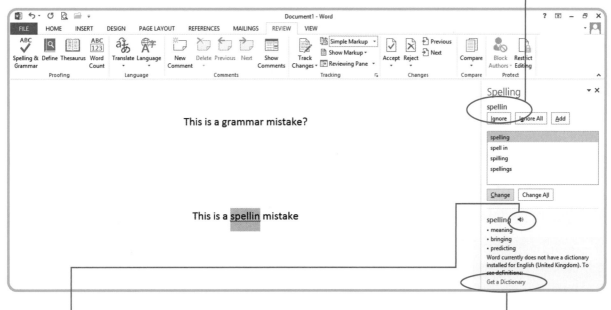

8 If an **audio icon** appears next to a word in the panel, click and you
will hear the word spoken or click **Get a Dictionary** to look it up.

Word links to the Internet to help
Research your work

**The Research pane finds information on the Internet. You can choose
from many different sources.**

1 Press the **Alt** key and click or click-and-drag the word(s) you want
more information about.

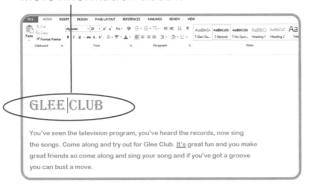

2 You will get a list of websites in the 'Research Pane'. Move this list
closer to your work using the **Task Pane Options** drop-down
menu button.

3 Scroll down the list and click on the website you want to check.

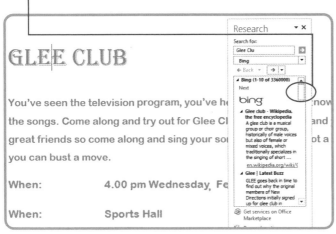

4 Click on a link to see that web page appear.

Party thank you project

Write well and find out more

Double check your *thank you* letter and research as you write.

1 Open a *thank you* letter, and click the **Spelling & Grammar** button on the **Review** tab.

2 Move the dialog box closer to the text using the **Task Pane Options** button.

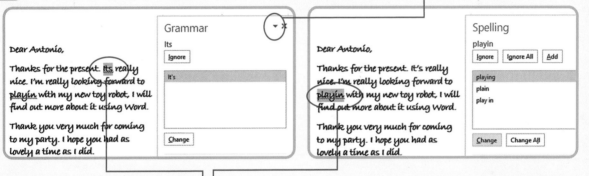

3 Check through all the underlined words until **Word** flashes 'Spelling and grammar check complete'.

4 Press the **Alt** key and click on on a word you want to find out more about.

5 Select a website from the list and click to open the web page.

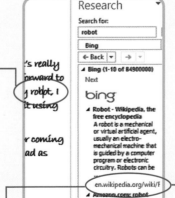

Collapse your work

It's useful to be able to hide lots of text sometimes.

The Collapse and Expand Headings function lets you fit really long essays into one page. You can use this in Read mode too.

1 Create a document with **multilevel** headings.

2 Hover the mouse-pointer near a heading. A gray triangle appears.

◢ Chapter 1 Mammals

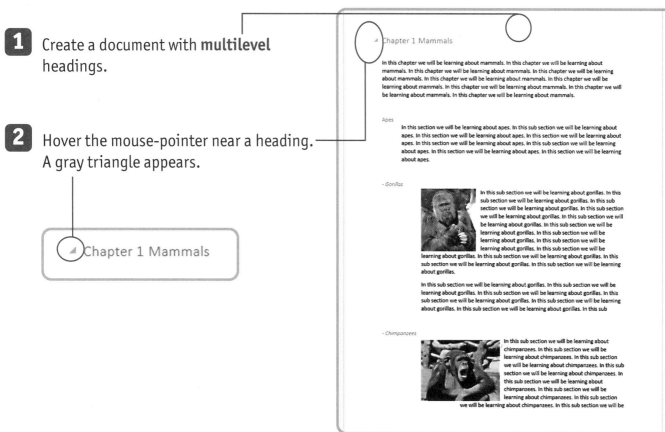

images: www.freeimages.co.uk

3 The triangle rotates and all the text that is covered by that heading disappears.

▷ Chapter 1 Mammals

Chapter 2 Fish

Sharks

- *Great White*

- *Tiger*

Fish

- *Freshwater*

- *Saltwater*

Chapter 3 Birds

Raptors

4 To close all the headings right-click on a heading and select **Collapse All Headings** from the drop-down menu.

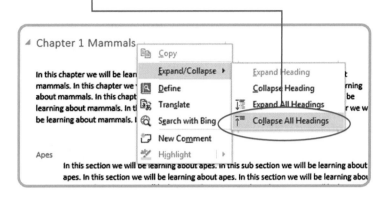

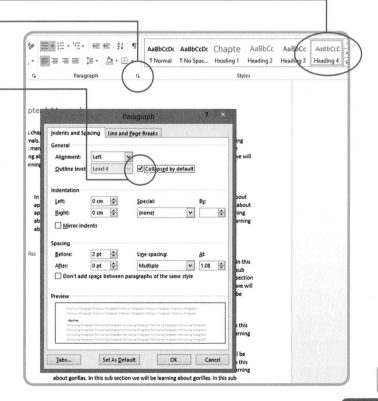

5 All the sub-headings will close and only the top level headings will be visible.

6 If you want your document to only show certain headings when it's opened, click on a **heading style** you want collapsed.

7 Then click on the **Paragraph toolset** button; a dialog box appears. Check the **Collapsed by default** box and press **OK**. All the headings of that style will collapse.

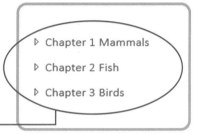

Top Tip!

To open all the headings, right-click on a heading and select **Expand All Headings** from the drop-down menu.

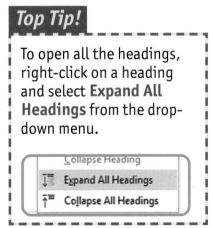

Navigate a Pane?

Using the Navigation Pane

The Navigation Pane quickly gets you to where you want to be in a long document.

1 Open your document with **multilevel** headings. Select **Expand All Headings** if they are collapsed.

2 On the **View** tab, click the **Navigation Pane** button.

3 Click **Headings** in the **Navigation Pane**. A list of the headings appears.

4 Select the heading you want to read about; **Word** displays that page.

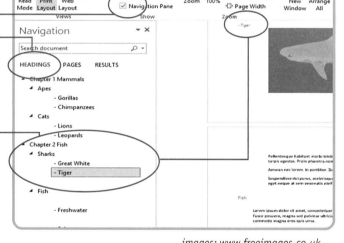

images: www.freeimages.co.uk

5 To see 'thumbnail' versions of each page, click on **Pages** in the **Navigation Pane**.

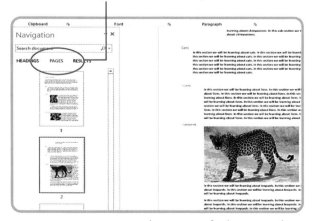

images: www.freeimages.co.uk

Top Tip!

Use the **Browse field** to find key words. Click on the word displayed and **Word** takes you to it.

Party thank you project

Make a super thank you book

Put all your *thank you* letters in one document and then Collapse and Navigate it.

1 Open all *thank you letters*. Copy and paste each one into a new document and save as *thank you book*. Add pictures.

2 Change every *Dear (first name)* to a heading style.

3 Right-click on a heading and select **Collapse All Headings** from the drop-down menu.

4 In the **View** tab, click the **Navigation Pane** button. The list of names appears.

5 Use the **Browse field** to find key words.

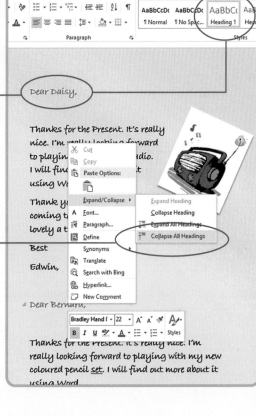

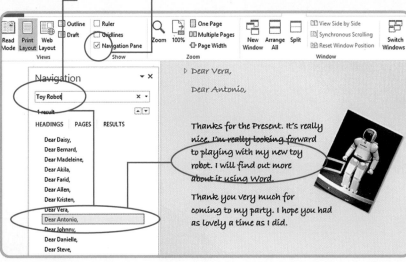

Saving online

Saving documents to the Cloud

Your work can be saved online; it saves space on your computer.

1 Open a document and click on the **File** tab. Select **Save As** and then your Cloud **OneDrive** location.

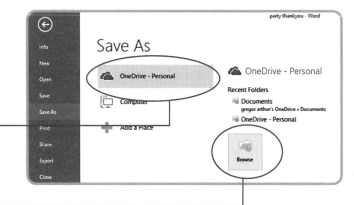

2 Click **Browse** to create a new online folder.

3 A dialog box appears with your **OneDrive folder** window. Create a **New folder** inside it. Save your document in this folder.

4 To open the file, select **Open** from the **File** tab background area. Then select the new **OneDrive folder**.

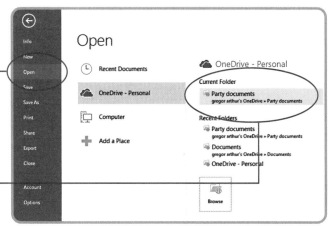

No Word?

Export, Open and edit PDFs

Your work can be viewed by someone who hasn't got Word. A PDF is a file that can be opened easily.

1 Open a document and select **Export** on the **File** tab. Then select **Create PDF/XPS Document** and press the button.

2 A dialog box appears. Make sure 'Save as type' is set to *PDF,* and click on the **Publish** button.

3 You can also open a **PDF**. Find and select the file in the usual way.

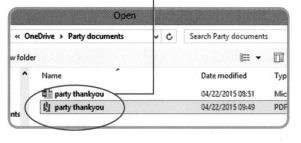

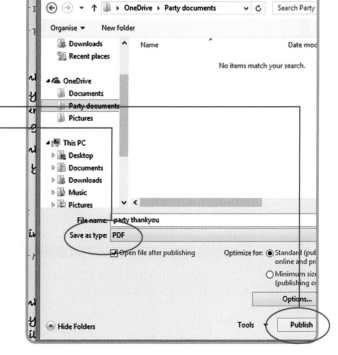

4 It may not look the same and styling may have changed but you can access and change the text.

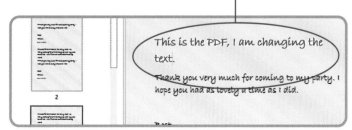

Present work online

Online Presentation is a great teamwork feature

You can show your work, live on the Internet, to other people via their web browsers.

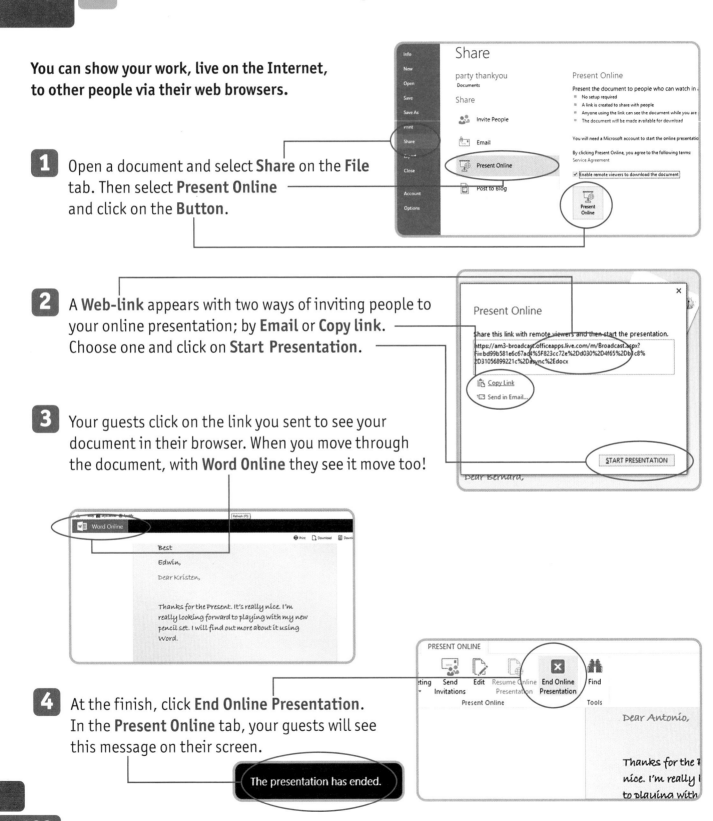

1 Open a document and select **Share** on the **File** tab. Then select **Present Online** and click on the **Button**.

2 A **Web-link** appears with two ways of inviting people to your online presentation; by **Email** or **Copy link**. Choose one and click on **Start Presentation**.

3 Your guests click on the link you sent to see your document in their browser. When you move through the document, with **Word Online** they see it move too!

4 At the finish, click **End Online Presentation**. In the **Present Online** tab, your guests will see this message on their screen.

The presentation has ended.

Campaign flyer project

Start your campaign online

You and your friends are starting a campaign with a flyer you have created. Present it to them online.

1 Create a *Healthy school lunch flyer*. Click on the **File** tab. Select **Save As** and then your Cloud **OneDrive** location.

2 Click **Browse** to create a new online folder named *Healthy school lunch*. Save the document.

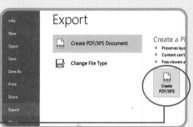

3 Select **Export** on the **File** tab. Select **Create PDF/XPS Document** and press the **Publish** button.

4 Save the **PDF** into the *Healthy school lunch* folder.

5 Select **Share** on the **File** tab, and then **Present Online**. Click on the **Button**.

6 Choose **Email** or **Copy link** and send the invite link to friends. Then click on **Start Presentation**.

7 Talk to your friends by phone or text while you show them parts of the flyer with **Word Online**.

Sharing online

Invite people to **Share** documents

If you need more people to help on your project, Share the document and everyone can work on one document, in one place.

1 Open a document and click on the **File** tab. Select **Save As** and **Add a Place** and then **Office 365 SharePoint** or **OneDrive**.

2 You will be asked to sign in to your account. Once that's done, create a folder location.

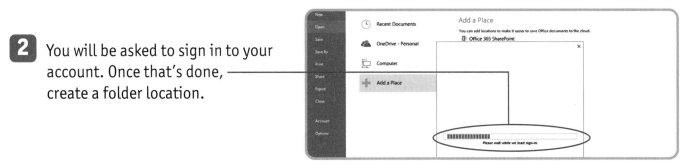

3 In the 'Save As' pane, your new location will appear. Save your file in your new location.

4 The first time you want to share a document online, select **Share** and **Invite People**. Then **Save to Cloud**.

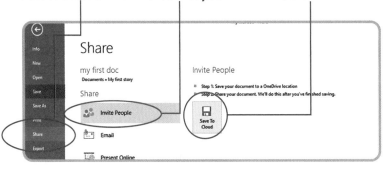

5 The **Invite People** pane appears. This is where you invite others to share.

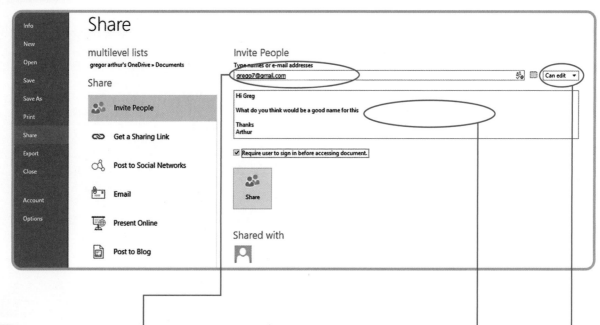

6 Type in **email addresses** for the people you are inviting to share.

7 Type an invite message into the **message field**.

8 Select **Can edit** or **Can view** from the drop-down menu.

9 Check if you want them to **sign in** with the password you give.
Then click on **Share**.

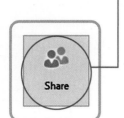

Get a sharing link

Using Sharing Links

Use Sharing Links to share a file to larger groups of people, by email or through social networks.

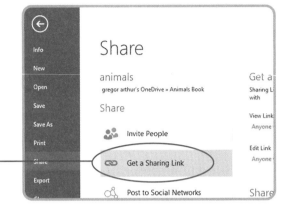

1 Open a document that has been saved online to **Onedrive** and select **Share** on the **File** tab.

2 Select **Get a Sharing Link**.

3 In the **Get a Sharing Link** pane there are two **Create Link** choices.

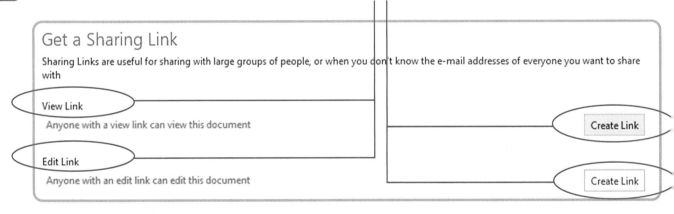

Get a Sharing Link

Sharing Links are useful for sharing with large groups of people, or when you don't know the e-mail addresses of everyone you want to share with

View Link

Anyone with a view link can view this document

Create Link

Edit Link

Anyone with an edit link can edit this document

Create Link

4 Create and copy the **Link** you want to send by selecting all (**Ctrl+A** keys).

View Link

https://onedrive.live.com/redir?page=view&resid=BD99B581E6C67AC4!472&authkey=!AEXjnNDoVB-33xl

Disable Link

5 Open your email and paste in the link (**Ctrl+V** keys). Add all of your friends' email addresses to make a group email.

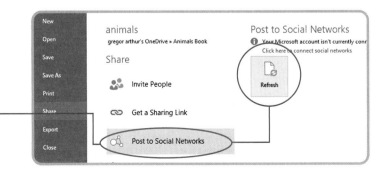

6 Or select **Share** and **Post to Social Networks**, but stay safe and make sure you know who can see the document.

Campaign flyer project

Let's all work on the flyer

Your friends want to help you work on the flyer. Use the Share pane to let them.

1 The first time you want to share the flyer online, select **Share** and **Invite People**. Then click the **Save to Cloud** button.

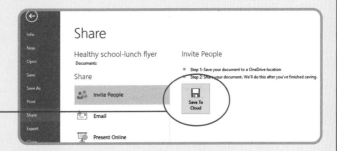

2 Type in **email addresses** for those you are inviting to share.

3 Type an invite message into the **message field**.

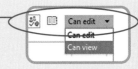

4 Select **Can edit** from the drop-down menu. Click on the **Share** button.

5 Select **Share** on the **File** tab. Then select **Get a Sharing Link**. Copy the **View link** and send to those who will be interested in your flyer but will not be working on it.

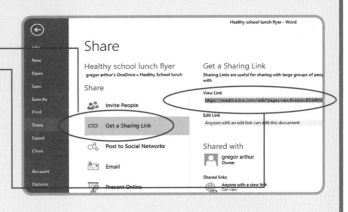

Can anybody help me?

You may be asked to **Comment** on a document by someone else.

Open the shared document on OneDrive.

1 Click on the **Review** tab and then the **Track Changes** button.

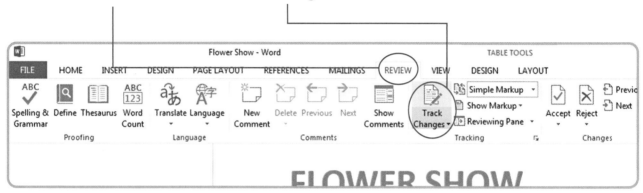

2 Try deleting text. You will see the deleted text is shown as **crossed out**. This is called 'Markup'.

3 Make changes to the words. Any text you add is marked as **underlined**.

4 To add a comment, highlight the text you want to comment on and click **New Comment**.

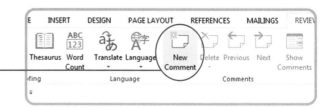

5 A **Comment box** appears at the side. Type in your comment.

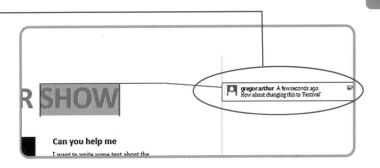

6 When you have finished, click anywhere outside the **Comment box**.

Can you help me

I want to write some text about the flower show. We made one big display in ~~a woodland~~ an urban setting, consisting of different varieties, some

7 If you are looking at someone else's changes you can accept them. **Highlight** the markup, then click on **Accept**. A list of options appears.

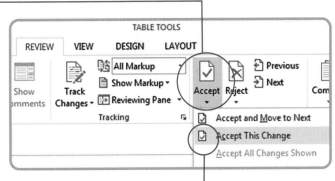

8 Click on **Accept This Change**. The text changes and the markup disappears.

flower show. We made one in an urban setting, consisting different varieties, some that bred ourselves, named after

Top Tip!

No need to print out and mark-up with a pen anymore. Save some paper, save some trees!

Help is always there

Did we lose you on one of
the projects?

Word has help built in. If you are connected to the
Internet there is even more help available.

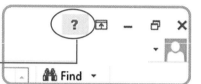

1 To get 'Help', click the **?** icon.

2 Type your question into the search field
and click **Search**.

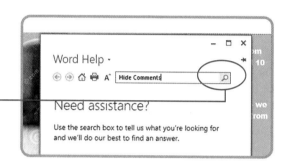

3 If you are on the Internet, **Help** will provide text and
video answers to your questions.

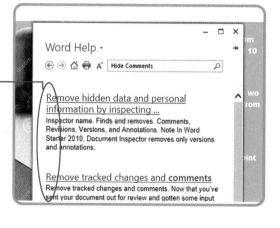

4 If the Internet connection is slow or not working, you
can change the connection status manually by clicking
on the button at the top of the pop-up.

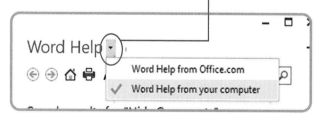

5 If you are not connected, you will see only help that is
built into the program.

Using the help menus project

Get yourself some help!

There are lots more tools to look at. Use Help to find out about them.

1 Search for help on the **Chart** button.

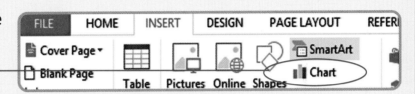

2 How can you add a **Hyperlink**?

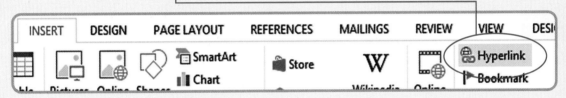

3 How do you **Hide Comments**?

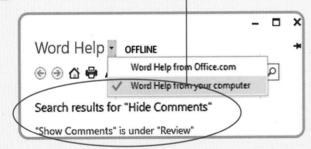

4 How can you stop other people changing your document?

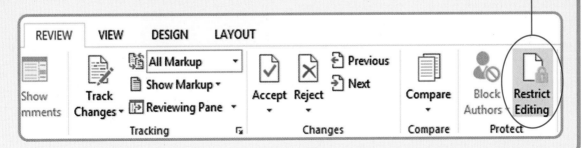

Index

ARCTURUS

This edition published in 2015 by Arcturus Publishing Limited
26/27 Bickels Yard, 151–153 Bermondsey Street,
London SE1 3HA

Copyright © Arcturus Holdings Limited

ISBN: 978-1-78599-096-0
AD004706US

Printed in China

Prepared for Arcturus by Starfish Design Editorial and Project Management Ltd.